GOD YES OR NO?

PHYSICS, FAITH,
AND SKEPTICISM

RON EDGE

CHARLIE POOLE

Edge

Publishing

RON EDGE | CHARLIE POOLE

GOD YES OR NO?

Copyright © 2015 Edge Publishing

EdgeFamilyPublishing.com

ISBN: 0996337911

ISBN-13: 978-0-9963379-1-5

TABLE OF CONTENTS

Introduction

It gives me great pleasure to introduce two highly regarded men of science as they cordially debate tenets of Christian faith. Dr. Charles Poole and his wife Kathleen, who originated from the bastions of Irish Catholic culture in New York, relocated to the heart of the Bible belt in Columbia S.C during the '60s when I was a child. My father, Dr. Ronald Edge, was already well established both as an experimental physicist at the University, and as a member of the lone Unitarian Fellowship in Columbia, which met in a small house on a residential street.

The main thing I knew about my dad while growing up was that he loved his work, and that he loved physics. He would collect toys that demonstrated principles of physics, enthusiastically performing demonstrations as far back as I can remember. Charlie, who had joined the same physics department, was a writing machine, spending every spare minute at the typewriter.

When you are a boy growing up in a physics environment, you don't think about your dad or associates as being particularly well known. Fortunately, I was able to appreciate the impact of both these men in the world of physics years later, when I decided to major in physics at college.

It was during a class in quantum mechanics that I was astounded to learn that an associate of my dad, Yakir Aharonov, whose small children I had once babysat, was cited in my textbook as a key discoverer of a well-known phenomenon known as the Aharonov-Bohm effect. This gave a new significance to his admonishment to me as a young lad years earlier: "Respect and appreciate your father; he is a brilliant man".

A few years later, as a physics grad student, I was on a bus with other physicists at a conference. The man next to me was a high school physics teacher, which is often a challenging profession due to the complete lack of equipment, support, or training. He conveyed to me that every physics teacher in America appreciated my dad because of his efforts helping high school physics teachers teach physics, by creating popular articles and a book entitled "String and Sticky Tape Experiments." As evidence of his labors, my dad was voted president of the American Association of Physics Teachers (AAPT), in whose monthly periodical his articles would appear.

Likewise, it was during my first summer of grad school while working as an assistant in a biophysics lab that the professor leading the group, Dr. Brill, became aware that I knew Charlie Poole. He was amazed that I was unaware of the fact that he was considered a leading world expert in the area of electron spin resonance or ESR, which is the basis for many key technologies, MRI in particular. "His famous book on ESR is **the** reference book on the subject – every physics library in America has at **least** one copy." Since that time, you only need to Google his name to find many reference books and textbooks on basic physics and research areas that grew out of his ESR work such as superconductivity.

The topic of religion first came up, as far as I am aware, a few years after Charlie's arrival. Charlie would drive the two of them to physics conferences, requiring many hours on the road. This would be fine except for the fact that apparently Charlie had slight narcoleptic tendencies, sometimes nodding off during a dinner only to wake up and pick up exactly where he left off. Being a bit concerned about this, my father would carefully watch Charlie while driving, and attempt to find ways to keep him awake and alert to avoid premature confirmation of whether there is life after death. My father soon discovered that bringing up certain religious topics such as the Virgin Birth, wherein he was quite pleased to play devil's advocate, was a most effective antidote for Charlie's sleepiness while driving.

It was no surprise to me therefore when Ron and Charlie announced that they were working together on a book debating the core beliefs of traditional Christianity. Charlie of course would explain (with help from his Jesuit training) various theological topics, adding his own unique perspective as a physicist. Ron would respond to Charlie's descriptions from a Unitarian perspective, with the added insight provided by his own knowledge of physics.

What is rather nice about this dialogue, I think, is that unlike so many such dialogues in today's polarized society, these two men know and respect each other. It is also fortunate that they both are in agreement on a very large subject area, namely physics and science in general. Neither will state their opinions and beliefs "just because" but rather will relate their faith worldview to their scientific worldview. Their conclusions may differ, but not due to being dogmatic nor due to lack of reason.

My hope is that this book will facilitate readers to think, regardless of their world-view or faith heritage. Believers should be cautious about rejecting scientific evidence. Likewise, non-believers should be cautious about rejecting matters of faith merely because they lie outside the realm of scientific discovery.

Dr. Christopher J. Edge

May 16, 2015

Chapter One

Worldview

Everyone has a worldview (or Weltanschauung in German) corresponding to his or her belief in what constitutes reality at its fundamental level of meaning. One of the authors of this book (RE) is a Unitarian physicist with a Scientific/Unitarian worldview based mainly on the laws of physics, and the other (CP) is a Catholic physicist with a Scientific/Christian worldview based mainly on the Christian faith. Both authors are retired physics professors who have spent their lives teaching and doing research, much of which involved directing the theses projects of graduate students working under their direction. Both had been very active in their respective churches.

At the present time the two most influential worldviews are the secular/scientific and the Christian, and they are contending or warring with each other and with Islam for dominance in the world. The secular/scientific view is held by many agnostics, atheists, Deists, Quakers, Unitarian/ Universalists, humanists, and other groups, while the particular Christian view presented here is shared by all the mainline churches (Anglican, Baptist, Catholic, Lutheran, Methodist, Mormon, Orthodox, Pentecostal, and Presbyterian). Christianity encompasses about 30% of the world's population while the secular scientific contingent is perhaps half as numerous in population but closer to equal in its ability to influence worldwide public opinion. The world is becoming more and more homogeneous in culture as it progresses through the 21st century, and how these two groups interact with each other will have a major influence on the nature of a possible future worldwide culture.

In this work the two physicists representing these two divergent ideologies will explain their respective viewpoints on over two dozen topics concerning a deity, democracy, the universe, life, mind/brain interactions, human aspirations, etc. On each topic one of the protagonists presents his position with some written comments and the other then provides a response to these comments. They alternate in presenting the initial point of view and in providing comments on and a response to this view. Their approaches to various topics are ordinarily quite different from each other, but they are not generally in conflict. In most cases they have simply different approaches. There are, of course, certain topics in which they have points of view that are strongly in disagreement or even diametrically opposed to each other, and these provide the reader with perhaps the most interesting discussions. In general, we mostly agree on the principles such as love thy neighbor, do not covert or damage. Where we differ refers mostly to the spiritual side of things. Is there a God? Even here there is some agreement. However, the definition of God is very tenuous and vague. After all, if you don't believe in God, how did we get here in the first place? Nevertheless, whether there is one God, or three, or a very large number is to many a superficial question, and to others of vital significance. We shall talk about this later.

Chapter Two

Why Do You Believe?

INITIAL COMMENTS BY RON

Why do people have a particular religion - or why not? The reasons are mixed and varied. The first and simplest reason is that I believe as my parents believe. So if *they* were Catholic, so am I. This leads to a close relationship with parents, and requires little thought. It also leads to the second reason - namely, to rebel against the parents - but then a decision must be made – what other church is suitable? I find many become Unitarians (UU) since UUs work out their own beliefs, and many new members come this way. Unfortunately, many of these members leave once have worked out what they really believe! My son, brought up a Unitarian, rebelled as a teenager by becoming a Catholic!

The second reason is to further one's political, economic, or social ends. If the socially elite are primarily Episcopalian, this is obviously the right belief. If most doctors and lawyers are Catholic in your town, and you sell them drugs or law books, then Catholicism is clearly your religion. There is a familiar English song called the Vicar of Bray, about a cleric who changed religion with that of the reigning monarch. There is not quite the same incentive in America, but nevertheless, there are ministers who bend their beliefs to fit their congregation. Often, they reach a point where they have to leave a church because bending is starting to reach a breaking point. They, too, often become Unitarians because of the broad spectrum of beliefs in their congregations.

Thirdly, but very rarely, one comes across someone who has genuine vision calling them to a particular belief. Such a one was St. Paul, originally Jewish, who received the call en route to Damascus.

REPLY BY CHARLIE

Ron gave us a very good overview of how various people arrive at their particular individual beliefs, so I will not contest what he wrote. His short essay prompts me to reminisce on how I arrived at and retained my own present beliefs. I initially inherited them from my Catholic parents, and they were continually reinforced by what I heard in Sermons at Mass and from the nuns in St. Gregory's grammar school. To my knowledge, none of my friends or neighbors exhibited any doubt. I spent four years of my youth reading the entire Bible to become knowledgeable on important beliefs. Then I read many of the church documents of the early centuries, mostly written by so-called Fathers of the Church like Augustine, and they reinforced my belief that the Catholic Church was the one True Church. Later some doubting arose when I realized the historical importance of the ancient adage *extra ecclesiam nulla salus* (outside the Church there is no salvation). It was hard for me to accept the viewpoint that the great majority of mankind, by not being Catholic, would not be saved. Eventually this was clarified at the Second Vatican Council (1962-1965):

> Whosoever, therefore, knowing that the Catholic Church was made necessary by God through Jesus Christ, would refuse to enter her or remain in her could not be saved. *Lumen Gentium* #14

> Those also can attain to everlasting salvation who through no fault of their own do not know the gospel of Christ or His Church, yet sincerely seek God and, moved by His grace, strive by their deeds to do His will as it is known to them through the dictates of their conscience. *LG* #16.

When I read these words, my doubts vanished. My journey of belief and the readings involved are presented on my website: www.faithseekingunderstanding.com.

For an academic and a scientist to truly believe in the truthfulness of Christianity there are some issues, which must be resolved. During our education we learn facts about history, plus facts about science, and the question arises as to the agreement between these various facts and what Scripture tells us. This secular learning must be reconciled with the inerrancy of scripture which is an important property of Scripture in both Catholic and Protestant traditions. The notion of inerrancy was clarified in 1965 at the Second Vatican Council in paragraph #11 of the Dogmatic Constitution on Divine Revelation (*Dei Verbum*)

> The books of Scripture must be acknowledged as teaching firmly, faithfully, and without error that truth which God wanted to be put into the sacred writings for the sake of our salvation.
>
> Therefore "all scripture is inspired by God." (2 Tim. 3:16).
>
> Thus inerrancy resulted from the sacred Scripture writers composing under the inspiration of the Holy Spirit.
>
> There are some cases in which details of historical events reported in the Scriptures are at variance with the corresponding accounts reported by reliable secular historians. The Scriptures could very well be in error historically since such details do not in any manner affect the religious teaching that is at stake, the latter being what is both inspired and inerrant.
>
> The writers of Genesis provide us with two creation stories related to ancient pagan myths. To understand these, we can interpret the word "day" as a symbol for

a long period of time. Some Christians suggested this during the early centuries of the Church.

Chapter Three

Science and Religion

INITIAL COMMENTS BY RON

The relationship between science and religion has presented a dilemma since science got its name. The problem is still not solved (if there is a solution), but it has provided delightful prospects for an argument over the years. By definition, religion is about why things happen, whereas science is about how they happen. The "how" part is straightforward and unambiguous, because it is based on experiment. If different experimenters get different results, something is wrong, and sooner or later other experimenters will find out why. Religion, on the other hand is very diverse - there are many important religions, and, even within the United States, thousands of less important ones. Most seek to send you to heaven, and many are convinced everyone else is going to hell. In spite of the fact they cannot all be right, one should not ignore them. My own feeling is, that if it gets you through the night, don't knock it, and the comfort provided by a suitable belief may preclude a detailed investigation. The principle point is, that your beliefs should not antagonize others, or cause harm to anyone.

WHAT DO SCIENTISTS BELIEVE?

Most scientists do not believe in a conventional god, although they do believe in something. James Watson, of DNA fame, said he only knew of one scientist who believed in a personal God, i.e. one who looked after you as an individual. That would be Francis Collins, (with whom I once sat on a committee), and who said the book "mere Christianity" by C.S. Lewis was what converted him (as it has many others). This book is from a series of talks delivered at the beginning of World War II by the British Broadcasting Corporation for a general audience, so they are very simple and straightforward.

What did some scientists believe?

Einstein believed the universe was too interesting not to have something involved, but not exactly a creator. "God does not throw dice," he said and also, "I cannot imagine a God who rewards and punishes the objects of his creation, whose purposes are modeled after our own - a God, in short, who is but a reflection of human frailty. Neither can I believe that the individual survives the death of his body, although feeble souls harbor such thoughts through fear or ridiculous egotism."

Thomas Jefferson said, "Religions are all alike – founded on fables and mythologies."

Bertrand Russell said, "Religion is based . . . mainly on fear . . . fear of the mysterious, fear of defeat, fear of death. Fear is the parent of cruelty, and therefore it is no wonder if cruelty and religion have gone hand in hand . . . My own view on religion is that of Lucretius. I regard it as a disease born of fear and as a source of untold misery to the human race."

SCIENCE AND RELIGION TODAY

How do science and religion mesh today? The contentions of the past are still with us, but most people who think differ from the outlook of the last century. Nevertheless, it is still true that scientists ask how, and prelates tell us why. The hope is the more we learn about the how, the closer we will really get to the why.

16

One thing on which scientists agree is that it is of prime importance to ask the right questions. We don't want to know how many angels dance on a pinhead. So what are the important questions? Firstly, such questions should be capable of a real answer, even if we don't know what it is. This means we should query first, "How did the universe start", and last such questions as, "Why are we here?" Short of a direct line to God (if there is a God) this question is currently unanswerable.

I have a quote from Harold Kroto, who was at my school and won the Nobel Prize for discovering a class of molecules called Bucky balls. He is now at Florida State: "I seek not the answer - but to understand the question." He actually attributes this to Buddha. He also suggested the John Templeton foundation give its next $1.5 million prize (more than the Nobel) for "progress in spiritual discoveries" to an atheist - Richard Dawkins, the famous Oxford professor, who wrote "The God Delusion" and said: "Faith is the great cop-out, the great excuse to evade the need to think and evaluate evidence. Faith is belief in spite of, even perhaps because of, the lack of evidence."

The most obvious questions, which have only recently been (at least partially) answered are, "Where did we come from, and where will we go?" Science has shown that the big bang is where we came from, and it is likely the universe will end with a vast expansion, where even atoms and nuclei blow apart (called "the big split"). Even these answers are subject to change, and, of course, people ask what happened before the big bang? The fact is, our knowledge about the nature of time is very restricted, so perhaps there was nothing before the big bang, or, on the other hand, it may be quite different from anything we have thought of. (Note I am ending with a preposition - scientists are allowed to do that). Roger Penrose has looked at recent experimental astronomical observations, and concluded we may be able to get some idea of what preceded the bang. Again, the nature of the end of the universe is subject to debate, but we are getting closer to what might happen, based on observing distant stellar explosions-supernova. Distance and time are tied together by the speed of light.

Another important question is what are we made of? Again, we know we are here to protect our DNA, which is a complex chemical, and of course our body is chemical-but how is consciousness tied up with this? How can we think about ourselves and particularly, how can we think about ourselves thinking

Someone I knew quite well in 1950 had anticipated Einstein in calculating how mass increased - (or more accurately "momentum increased") with speed - what we now call "special relativity". That was G. F. C. Searle at the Cavendish lab – J. J. Thompson's colleague. He was the supreme eccentric who held strong religious views, possibly having been cured of a disease by Christian Science during WW I. [See: G.F.C Searle, Phil. Mag., 1897, 340]

About religion, Charles Darwin said, "I feel most deeply that the whole subject is too profound for the human intellect. A dog might as well speculate on the mind of Newton". I had an oral exam in Darwin's room in Christ's college at Cambridge. I failed miserably, but did OK subsequently. So did Darwin.

J. B. S. Haldane, a famous biologist, said in 1934, "My practice as a scientist is atheism - that is to say, in setting up an experiment, I assume no god, angel or devil is going to interfere with its course; and this assumption has been justified by such success as I have achieved in my professional career." Haldane also said: "All I can say is that the Almighty showed an inordinate fondness for beetles," in reply to a theologian who asked him what God was like.

People sometimes try to score debating points by saying,

"Evolution is only a theory." That is correct, but it's important to understand what that means. It is also only a theory that the world goes round the sun -- it's just a theory for which there is an immense amount of evidence. There are many scientific theories that are in doubt, and even within evolution there is some room for controversy. But that we are cousins of apes, jackals, and starfish, is a fact in the ordinary sense of the word. (Richard Dawkins, from "Nick Pollard interviews Richard Dawkins," Damars: 1999).

Thoreau said, "The boy gathers materials for a temple, and then when he is thirty, concludes to build a woodshed."

Humanists (secular or not), logical positivists, and now philosophical theists (who used to be called Deists, who believe in God but deny revealed religion) often think that God exists independent of the teaching or revelation of any particular religion. This is frequently what scientists feel, but seldom express.

> Consider the Anthropic Principle, which comes in weak and strong formulations. With respect to the question: "Why are we here?" this principle may give a hint which is of extreme importance, but we rarely hear of it because philosophers and theologians don't understand it, and physicists would rather be doing something else. The weak variety states:
>
> The observed values of all physical and cosmological quantities are not equally probable but they take on values restricted by the requirement that there exist sites where carbon-based life can evolve and by the additional requirement that the universe be old enough for it to have already done so.

In other words, we are here, and we are carbon-based life, so this biases our view of the universe. It does not mean that the universe was created for us, but it does mean **we can only**

19

comprehend a universe where we can exist.

It might be worthwhile inserting here a reference to the political fight over whether to put intelligent design ("creationism in a cheap tuxedo") in the school science curriculum. The formula for our DNA shows experimentally and conclusively that 90% of our genes are the same as those in fruit flies and amoebae, and an even larger fraction is present in the hominid apes. Why, then should we wonder about evolution, when this even greater wonder is right before our eyes?

REPLY BY CHARLIE

In his initial comments Ron made some very interesting observations on the topic of science and religion. He claimed that most scientists do not believe in a conventional god. In actuality the percentage of scientists who belong to various religions is probably comparable to that of other professions. For example, several well known scientists, some of whose statements or publications indicate a belief in a personal God are: Stephen M. Barr (Modern Physics and Ancient Faith), Francis S. Collins (The Language of God), Pierre Duhem (Thermodynamics and Chemistry), Stanley L. Jaki (Brain, Mind and Computers), Blaise Pascal (The Geometrical Spirit), Arthur A. Peacocke (Chaos and Complexity), John Polkinghorne (The Faith of a Physicist), Pierre Teilhard de Chardin (The Phenomenon of Man), and Frank J. Tipler (The Anthropic Cosmological Principle).

There are organizations of scientists who are Christians that involve themselves in various activities such as sponsoring workshops and conventions and publishing newsletters, journals, and books on Christian approaches to scientific issues. An example is the American Scientific Affiliation (ASA), which hosts conferences and publishes the monthly journal <u>Perspectives on Science and Christian Faith.</u> Another such organization is the Institute for Theological Encounter with Science and Technology (ITEST) that sponsors an annual conference on a particular topic and afterwards publishes the proceedings of the conference with the text of each talk and the interchanges during the discussion session after each talk. The latter are particularly enlightening. The University of Chicago hosts a similar organization that publishes the journal Zygon.

I consider the suggestion of Harold Kroto that Richard Dawkins be awarded the next Templeton Prize for "progress in spiritual discoveries" as ludicrous. In the *God Delusion* Dawkins wrote the following on page 31:

> The God of the Old Testament is arguably the most unpleasant character in all fiction: jealous and proud of it; a petty, unjust, unforgiving, control-freak; a vindictive bloodthirsty ethnic cleanser; a misogynistic, homophobic, racist, infanticidal, genocidal, filicidal, pestilential, megalomaniacal, sadomasochistic, capriciously malevolent bully.

Someone who wrote this certainly has no right to a Templeton Prize.

In July 2007 the Scientific American published a "debate" on the subject "Should Science Speak to Faith" in which the two protagonists were the avowed atheistic scientists Richard Dawkins and Lawrence Krauss. I as a Christian scientist was appalled by the idea of two scientists who are hostile to Faith "debating" this issue. If a well-respected theological journal were to publish a debate on the subject "Should Faith Speak to Science" and the two protagonists in the debate were theologians both of whom are hostile to science the academic world would be loud and emphatic in its denunciation of such a display of hypocrisy by leaders of the Christian community. The editors of Scientific American declined to publish the letter of protest submitted by biology Professor Austin Hughes and myself.

I become disturbed when I read comments by detractors of religion such as Bertrand Russell and Richard Dawkins about alleged miseries inflicted on mankind by religion. The Gospels, and especially the Sermon on the Mount recounted in Chapters 5 to 7 of Matthew are very clear when they assert: "Blessed are the peacemakers" and "Love your enemies, and pray for those who persecute you." The sentiments expressed in this Sermon are unique to Christianity, and demonstrate that it is truly the religion of peace.

Chapter Four

Christianity and Unitarianism

CHRISTIANITY BY CHARLIE

Jesus Christ was born in Bethlehem approximately 4 BC and died by crucifixion near Jerusalem approximately 33 AD. Shortly after the resurrection of Jesus his disciples, aided by St. Paul, founded the Christian Church and it spread rapidly throughout Palestine, Asia Minor, Greece, and other regions, eventually reaching Rome where Peter and Paul were martyred; The Church underwent successive persecutions for two or three centuries until the Edict of Milan proclaimed by Constantine in 313 AD, and in 380 AD it became the religion of the Roman Empire. In the year 393 AD a Council convened at Hippo in North Africa decided upon the 27 books that constitute the New Testament Scriptures. Several books had been in dispute up to that time.

During the first three or four centuries there were disputes in the Church about the nature of God and the nature of Jesus so General (Ecumenical) Councils or assemblies of bishops were convened at Nicaea (325 AD), Constantinople (383). Ephesus (431) and Chalcedon (451) to decide these questions. The Council of Nicaea formulated a declaration called the Nicene Creed, which was modified at the second Ecumenical Council. This Creed summarizes the main official fundamental beliefs of Christianity, and reads as follows:

Nicene Creed

We believe in one God, the Father, the almighty,

maker of heaven and earth, of all that is seen and unseen. We believe in one Lord, Jesus Christ, the only Son of God, eternally begotten of the Father, God from God, Light from Light, true God from true God, begotten, not made, one in being with the Father. Through him all things were made. For us men and for our salvation he came down from heaven, by the power of the Holy Spirit he was born of the Virgin Mary, and became man. For our sake he was crucified under Pontius Pilate, he suffered died and was buried. On the third day he rose again in fulfillment of the scriptures; He ascended into heaven and is seated at the right hand of the Father. He will come again in glory to judge the living and the dead and his kingdom will have no end. We believe in the Holy Spirit the Lord and giver of life, who proceeds from the Father and **the Son,** with the Father and the Son is worshiped and glorified. He has spoken through the prophets. We believe in one holy catholic and apostolic Church. We acknowledge one Baptism for the forgiveness of sins. We look for the resurrection of the dead and the life of the world to come.

There are other creeds in the Church such as the very short Apostles' Creed and the much longer Athanasian Creed. They all say basically the same things.

As scientists we can ask the question "Is there structure in God?" This is similar to asking the question "Is there structure in water and ice?" The answer to the second question is that if you observe at higher and higher magnifications both water and ice consist of water molecules, and this molecule consists of two atoms of hydrogen (H) and one of oxygen (O). Under higher magnification the hydrogen atom consists of a proton surrounded by an electron cloud and the oxygen consists of eight protons bound to eight neutrons plus eight orbiting electrons. The protons and neutrons in turn are made of quarks. From the viewpoint of biology an animal consists of many organs, and each organ in turn consists of tissues, with each tissue in turn consisting of smaller cells. A cell has a nucleus and surrounding cytoplasm, and so on, etc. The first four Ecumenical Councils decided that there is indeed structure in the one God since He consists of a Trinity of three divine persons called the Father, the Son and the Holy Spirit, all equal with the same divine nature. Jesus Christ the Son became incarnate (acquired humanity) of the Virgin Mary so He has two natures, one human and one divine. . He suffered and died on the cross to redeem mankind from their sins. On the third day He rose from the dead, and then 40 days later (went) ascended back to heaven. These fundamental beliefs, which are summarized in the Creeds, plus all the decrees of the first four Ecumenical Councils are acknowledged by all the mainline churches or denominations of Christianity: Anglican (Episcopalian), Baptist, Catholic, Lutheran, Orthodox, and Presbyterian.

During the first few centuries the Christian Church tried hard to keep itself united. However From time to time divergent or heretical views would become widespread with separate churches sometimes forming. For example the Arians claimed that Jesus was not truly God and the Iconoclasts attacked the veneration of images. Eventually these early heresies died out, and until the year 1054 AD the Church remained more or less fairly united under the Pope. Then in the year 1054 the Eastern Schism took place when the Eastern branch of the Church centered at Constantinople separated from the Western branch centered at Rome with the jurisdiction of the pope no longer recognized in the east. The main doctrinal difference was that the Eastern Church did not acknowledge the bold faced words in the Creed "from the Son," *filioque* in Latin, as belonging in the Creed. The Schism persists to the present time.

The sixteenth century saw the break-up of Western Christendom into several rival churches such as the Anglican (Episcopalian), Lutheran, and Presbyterian denominations, with the Baptists appearing a little later in time. These Protestant Reformation Churches accept the Creeds and the authenticity of the first four Ecumenical Councils, and they emphasize the adage *sola scriptura* or Scripture only for deciding upon accepting doctrines. Eastern Orthodoxy was unaffected by the Protestant Reformation, and accepts the first seven Ecumenical Councils. Catholicism accepts 21 Ecumenical Councils, the most recent one Vatican II having been in session from 1962 through 1965. These newly formed Protestant churches have persisted to the present time, and the 20th century witnessed the rise of a new version of Christianity called Pentecostalism. All of these various churches are sufficiently close in belief and in practice so that from the perspective of the present book they constitute a single worldview called Christianity.

REPLY BY RON

The Christian message had many advantages in being disseminated, as Poole has shown. Firstly, the message of love is very appealing (however badly carried out in practice!). Although the Jewish population was small and poor in Christ's time, they were very religious, and willing to listen. The conquest by the Romans, at first sight a catastrophe for the Jews, benefitted the Christians, in that the Romans were endeavoring to suppress Judaism in favor of their own religion. This left an opening for Christianity. When Christianity caught on, the Roman communications network-roads seaways etc. meant that Christianity could be spread around with ease, as St Paul found out-in fact Paul was the ideal disciple. Later, the emperor Constantine realized it would be better to join the Christians than fight them, and it became the religion of the empire. As with all established organizations, it deteriorated and split up with time, so today we have a vast number of religions calling themselves "Christian" many with ideals and doctrines Christ would have frowned upon. Nevertheless, the basic concepts of Christianity remain. There are two great commands. The first is from the *Shema*: Dt 6:4 (The Jewish morning and evening prayer service) "Hear, O Israel, the Lord our God is one Lord; and you shall love the Lord your God with all your heart, and with all your soul, and with all your might." (Note it states, "one Lord"). The second is "You shall love your neighbor as yourself". "On these two commandments depend all the law and the prophets."

This represents the basis of the Christian religion, and psychologically is the basis of what humanity requires to survive. We must have something to believe in, and this is it. The first commandment is not quite what modern civilization believes in, however, being a bit too mystical. Nevertheless, even today we would like to have a specific reason for living.

Christianity has appropriated a large share of the world's religious population of the present time. It is interesting to see, however, the great similarity it has to the other religions of about the time of its foundation. The Virgin Birth, ascension into heaven, reappearance etc. can be found in many other religions, frequently religions with no direct connection with Christianity. Why is this? To some extent it is likely because evolution has left us with brains that demand answers to certain fundamental questions - where did we come from, where will we go, why are we here? - and provided a preview of the answers to these questions which eventuated in Christianity. As with all evolutionary solutions, the losers faded away or were incorporated, as for example Easter was originally a pagan celebration. We did not have the scientific knowledge we have today at the time of Christ, but our social needs were just the same. Thus it is that the two simple demands of Christianity - love thy neighbor and love thy God - still make up the basis of Christianity even if there are many other demands upon our credulity - for example, the Trinity "Three in one, and one in three".

It pays to be somewhat ambiguous about what we mean by "God". To some it may mean a tyrant sitting on a throne demanding obedience, to others, a loving being giving out hugs. Over the years the concept of a multiplicity of Gods has given way to a single being, covering a variety of attributes.

It is interesting to speculate what would have happened to Christianity if Christ had been born today. On the one hand, modern digital electronic communication techniques would have made the dissemination of Christ's ideas virtually instantaneous. On the other hand, our knowledge of the physical universe is so much in advance of what was known in Christ's time that many of his concepts would have been found not relevant - such items as healing the sick, when a dose of antibiotic would be prescribed today! Nevertheless, his basic ideas are as relevant today as they were then.

UNITARIANISM BY RON

Charlie has mentioned why he is a Christian, but I haven't said why I am a Unitarian, or what Unitarianism is. I was christened a Methodist, confirmed in the Church of England, and married in the Anglican church of Australia (to a lapsed Catholic), my second marriage being in the Unitarian church in Florida (to a lapsed Lutheran). I had always had strong belief doubts in the Christian church primarily in connection with such things as the virgin birth, miracles such as the loaves and fishes, the ascension into heaven etc. The moral precepts put forward by Christ seemed to me to be fine.

Unitarians always have a hard time saying what they believe in. It is much easier to say what they don't have to believe in, because Unitarians have no specific creed, like conventional Christians. It is up to each Unitarian to come to his or her own beliefs. We had a competition once for what we would tell someone in an elevator between floors, what Unitarianism is. The "elevator definition." We came to the conclusion we would say, "we are the "no hell" church". This may be a bit sketchy, and certainly I am sure some would disagree with it, but it has some truth. Another saying provides the difference between Unitarians and Universalists - Unitarians were too good for God to damn, and Universalists felt God was too good to damn man. Hence, we have members of the Unitarian church who are agnostics and even atheists. With such a diverse group, perhaps it is a good idea to briefly examine their history, and see how they got that way.

The first question most people ask is - are Unitarians Christians? This question would have been much easier to answer a hundred years ago and it would have been "yes" (although many would disagree, since the "Trinity" would be absent, but Christ would still be deemed divine). However, since Unitarians have no creed, so their beliefs can change, and over the years they have become less "Christian", by which I mean, they take Christ as a normal human being with some bright ideas, rather than being divine.

One of the first Unitarians was the Egyptian Pharaoh Akhenaten 1350 BC. He altered the beliefs of all previous rulers of Egypt to a monotheistic God, associated with the sun. It didn't last. The Romans believed in many Gods, particularly their emperors. After much argument the Christians came to believe in a "Trinity", a curious concept I never quite understood, with three persons in one God. However, they balked at allowing any divergence from their creed, burning those who disagreed. In1531 the Spaniard Michael Servetus published "On the Errors of the Trinity" and in 1553, "The Restoration of Christianity", being executed in the same year. Socinianism was a Unitarian doctrine formulated by the Italian Lelio Socinus (from the "radical reformation") and promulgated in the 1550s. This was probably when one might say the modern view of Unitarianism began. In1568, at the Diet of Torda a religious toleration act was passed. Unitarianism began in Transylvania under Francis David and in1571 Unitarianism was recognized as an official "received religion" there. Unfortunately, in 1572 King Sigismund of Transylvania (who had supported Unitarianism) died and that same year Unitarianism was banned. In 1579, Francis David died.

During the period of the reformation, religious ideas were in somewhat of a turmoil, so in 1662 the "Great Ejection" followed the passage of the act of Uniformity by the British Parliament. The act was supposed to force the people to conform to one religion. In fact what it did was to encourage immigration to America, where the religion laws were much more tolerant, South Carolina in particular providing few restrictions, as witness the Huguenot church still going strong in Charleston. In England, the "Five mile act" prevented Unitarians from congregating within five miles of any city. In 1655, John Biddle (the "father" of English Unitarianism) was banished from England for his views. However, in1689 things eased a little, and the Toleration Act gave Dissenters more freedom. In 1774 Theophilus and Hannah Lindsey founded the first Unitarian congregation in England at the Essex Street Chapel, by the Strand in London. In 1794, after his home had been attacked by rioters, Joseph Priestley and his family left England and settled in America near Philadelphia starting a Unitarian group. It is worthwhile noting that of the first four presidents of the United States, three were Unitarian, but they did not proselytize, so Unitarians were few! Although historically Unitarianism is associated with Transylvania in the 16th century, modern Unitarianism in America comes more from a split in the Congregational church of the early nineteenth century. The Congregationalists have a creed differing from the orthodox in that they believe one can only communicate with God through the medium of Christ and not directly. Unitarians of course hold no such doctrine. Calvinists also believe in predestination, so bad or good, we cannot change the future. The doctrinal fight was basically between Calvinists and Unitarians. The Calvinists believe the doctrines of scripture are the only rule of faith, and in the bondage of human free will through sin, and the justification by grace through faith.

American Unitarianism came out of the Massachusetts congregational churches, which organized themselves around the principles articulated in the Cambridge Platform of 1648. This document was created to settle differences between local congregations on matters of church discipline and to explain themselves to the Church of England, to which they all professed to belong. Doctrinally consistent with the Reformation Christianity of the day, the Platform sought to prove that Congregationalism was the best and most biblically accurate form of church governance, so it was less on the dogma and more on the church organization that they differed from other dissenters - for example they had no conventional hierarchy, no bishops, archbishops etc.

The Cambridge Platform holds that "there is no greater Church than a Congregation," which consists of visible "saints" (members of the congregation) in voluntary agreement and covenant with each other to "worship, edify and have fellowship." Each church is autonomous, because there is no higher authority than the congregation. And yet the Platform also says:

"This government of the church is a mixed government... In respect to Christ, the head and king of the church, it is a monarchy: In respect of the body, or Brotherhood of the church... it resembles a democracy. In respect of the Presbytery [sic] and power committed to them, it is an Aristocracy"

Although the general description of the government of the congregational church sounds foreign, some of the details are familiar, such as granting members the right to determine their own leaders and standards of membership.

The Unitarian movement grew principally in New England, although Washington and Philadelphia had early congregations, and Charleston in South Carolina got its first Unitarian minster in 1817, the church itself not being termed

"Unitarian" until 1839. Harvard University was the source of much controversy in the early days. The problem arose in picking a new president and Professor in Divinity. Ultimately Unitarians were chosen for both posts, although the more conservative Calvinistic contenders came close to winning.

The mid nineteenth century might well be termed the "Golden Age of Unitarianism". The sect had found its feet and became an accepted faith, even if they were not clear exactly what that faith was. It was certainly not the faith we see today.

Up to the 1830s and '40s Unitarians held that religion, specifically liberal religion, should be ultimately rational. Then a "New school" of religious liberals called "Transcendentalists" began to insist otherwise. They claimed religion was properly a matter of intuition, emotion and faith. This controversy ran high, though its importance is not seen today. Ultimately schism was avoided, and compromise reached. Many famous people were transcendentalists - Ralph Waldo Emerson, Theodore Parker, Henry David Thoreau, George Bancroft, and Margaret Fuller among them.

Unitarians and Universalists have long had a close relationship. After much discussion in1962 they merged. Universalists tend not to proselytize, with the result that their numbers have been dwindling, so the merger probably benefitted both religions.

Today, UUs hold many and varied beliefs. The membership grew by 15.8% from 2000 to 2010, but is still small at about 211,000. The growth is more rapid in the South at the new congregations, many of which started in the '50s as "fellowships". With increasing knowledge in scientific discoveries, such as evolution and molecular biology (DNA) it is likely this growth will persist into the future.

Chapter Five

Einstein and Newton

INTIAL COMMENTS BY CHARLIE

Albert Einstein (1879-1955) lived about two generations or half a century before the authors of the present book. In 1949, five years before his death, the *Library of Living Philosophers* published Volume VII entitled *Albert Einstein: Philosopher - Scientist.*

This volume began with Autobiographical Notes by Einstein, followed by fifteen descriptive and critical essays on his work, which Einstein then commented upon. His only mention of religion was a short remark at the beginning (p. 3) of these notes. He asserted "the traditional educational machine" gave him "a deep religiosity" as a young child despite his being "the son of entirely irreligious (Jewish) parents ... this found an abrupt ending at the age of 12. Through the reading of popular science books I soon reached the conviction that much of the stories of the Bible could not be true." There followed "a positively fanatic orgy of freethinking ... a crushing impression ... Suspicion against every kind of authority grew out of this experience." Throughout his life Einstein never associated himself with any church. The final contributor to *Volume VII of Living Philosophers*, Virgil Hinshaw, quoted Einstein on page 659 as saying "I believe in Spinoza's God who reveals Himself in the orderly harmony that exists, not in a God who concerns himself with fates and actions of Human beings. Carl Seelig (in *Ideas and Opinions, Albert Einstein*, p. 48) says "His religious feeling takes the form of a rapturous amazement at the harmony of natural law, which reveals an intelligence of such superiority that, compared with it, all the systematic thinking and acting of human beings is an utterly insignificant reflection." Max Jammer in his book *Einstein and Religion* considers Einstein's statement "Science without religion is lame and religion without science is blind" as the epitome of his philosophy of religion. He quoted further "Subtle is the Lord, but malicious He is not." Basically Einstein believed in a transcendent creator God, but not in a personal God. He did, however, admire Jesus as the person depicted in the New Testament.

It is gratifying to learn that Einstein did believe in God. This provides a good counterbalance to those scientists who not only fail to believe, but who are militant in their disbelief. They are anxious to convince the entire world of their claim that science demonstrates that God does not exist. They seek to remove the phrase "in God we trust" from all U. S. Currency and the phrase "under God" from the U. S. Pledge of Allegiance to the Flag. They seek to ban signs with any reference to religion from public property, and any recital of prayer in public schools. These militant atheists have no way of proving that God does not exist, and their viewpoint is contrary to that of the great majority of mankind. We rejoice in Einstein's conviction that the Creator-God does exist!

REPLY BY RON

It is interesting to examine not only Einstein's beliefs but also that of others - specifically famous scientists such as Newton, and Watson and Crick because of the effects of their discoveries

The treatment of Einstein's beliefs has been dealt with extensively by Walter Isaacson in his book. It seemed to me pretty obvious what Einstein believed in was what Charlie says. He clearly did not believe in a conventional personal god for a very specific reason. Why would God set up a universe with laws, which were incapable of being changed in the slightest without the collapse of everything like a house of cards, then proceed to intervene in the lives lived by the participants of this system? The whole concept of physical laws is very demanding mathematically. Nevertheless, Einstein believed in a deterministic universe. This view is rarely held by physicists. The reason is, of course, that it does away with free will. There are ways of getting around this, but most of them are specious.

Newton had an interesting religious background. He was appointed Lucasian professor at Cambridge (later held by Dirac and Hawking) which demanded he be a conventional Church of England Christian. However, there is much evidence he held Unitarian views which he was at considerable pains to conceal. The first part of his adult life he spent examining the possibility of magical and esoteric views of the universe, before he became involved in the genuine physics of mechanics (gravity) and light. He was of a rather unpleasant and argumentative disposition, so had few friends, but his abilities were such that he was able to keep his chair, though he ultimately had a stroke and later became master of the mint, where he had several individuals executed for forgery. He said, "Nature does nothing in vain when less will serve; for Nature is pleased with simplicity and affects not the pomp of superfluous causes". This resembles Occam's razor which states: "Among competing hypotheses that predict equally well, the one with the fewest assumptions should be selected. Other, more complicated solutions may ultimately prove to provide better predictions, but—in the absence of differences in predictive ability—the fewer assumptions that are made, the better."

Maynard Keynes wrote a very interesting and insightful dissertation on Newton.

It is perhaps worthwhile examining the beliefs of Watson and Crick, since it is their discovery of the structure of DNA which has lead to our understanding of how "life" occurs. Crick referred to himself as a humanist, which he defined as the belief "that human problems can and must be faced in terms of human moral and intellectual resources without invoking supernatural authority." Crick once joked, "Christianity may be OK between consenting adults in private but should not be taught to young children." He publicly called for humanism to replace religion as a guiding force for humanity, writing:

"I do not respect Christian beliefs. I think they are ridiculous. If we could get rid of them, we could more easily get down to the serious problem of trying to find out what the world is all about...The human dilemma is hardly new. We find ourselves through no wish of our own on this slowly revolving planet in an obscure corner of a vast universe. Our questioning intelligence will not let us live in cow-like content with our lot. We have a deep need to know why we are here. What is the world made of? More important, what are we made of? In the past religion answered these questions, often in considerable detail. Now we know that almost all these answers are highly likely to be nonsense, having sprung from man's ignorance and his enormous capacity for self-deception... The simple fables of the religions of the world have come to seem like tales told to children. Even understood symbolically they are often perverse, if not rather unpleasant... Humanists, then, live in a mysterious, exciting and intellectually expanding world, which, once glimpsed, makes the old worlds of the religions seem fake - cozy and stale... "

In 1960, Crick accepted an honorary fellowship at Churchill College, Cambridge, one factor being that the new college did not have a chapel.

The antipathy to religion of the DNA pioneers is long standing. In 1961 Crick resigned his fellowship of Churchill College, when it proposed to build a chapel.

When Sir Winston Churchill wrote to him pointing out that "none need enter [the chapel] unless they wish", Crick replied that on those grounds, the college should build a brothel, and enclosed a cheque for 10 guineas.

"My hope is that eventually it will be possible to build permanent accommodation within the college, to house a carefully chosen selection of young ladies in the charge of a suitable Madam who, once the institution has become traditional, will doubtless be provided, without offence, with dining rights at the High Table," he wrote.

Watson is an atheist. In 2003, he was one of 22 Nobel Laureates who signed the Humanist Manifesto:

- Knowledge of the world is derived by observation, experimentation, and rational analysis.
- Humans are an integral part of nature, the result of unguided evolutionary change
- Ethical values are derived from human need and interest as tested by experience
- Ethical values are derived from human need and interest as tested by experience
- Life's fulfillment emerges from individual participation in the service of humane ideals.
- Humans are social by nature and find meaning in relationships
- Working to benefit society maximizes individual happiness

Watson's outspoken remarks about the intellectual ability of different races have left him much trouble.

It is not clear what these people mean by "atheist", since their definition of God is not clear. This highly organized universe has more than a random creation. So what does this mean? Clearly not a God sitting on a throne with a long white beard, but something created the orderliness we see all around.

Chapter Six

Where Did I Come from and Where Will I Go?

INITIAL COMMENTS BY RON

When I was in grade school we had little knowledge of these topics. In fact, the size and age of the universe were still mysteries. Now we have a pretty good picture of its origins and potential endings. But this still leaves a lot that we don't know. By the time I was an undergraduate in the 1950's the fight was on between Fred Hoyle, and George Gamow about the start. Hoyle believed in the continuous creation of matter, so the universe had always been the same. Gamow believed in what Hoyle called the "big bang". Both agreed on the expanding universe, but Hoyle preferred to keep the density constant, matter was being created continuously, whereas Gamow believed the universe started at an immensely dense point, which then exploded like a bomb. Hoyle and Gamow were interesting characters, whom I got to know over the years. Hoyle was a bluff, no-nonsense Yorkshire man with a strong accent. Gamow was a Russian with a very well developed sense of humor.

The problem was solved with the discovery of the microwave background radiation that fills the whole universe and could only have come from the explosion of the original microscopic source - a "singularity". Since then, more and more has been learned. For example, we now believe that an inflationary period of growth occurred 10^{-36} seconds after the "Bang" singularity, finishing about 10^{-32} seconds later, with the universe having increased in size by 10^{78} times. This was followed by a more normal expansion, ending in our present configuration. This inflation explains why the universe is flat, homogeneous, and isotropic (i.e. uniform in all directions). However, these rather esoteric cosmological problems don't affect our everyday life! Our satellite telescopes of various kinds allow us to observe the structure of the universe at all wavelengths of the electromagnetic spectrum, up to a distance and time limit provided by the big bang some 13.75 billion years ago, and many light years away. We can now follow the probable life history of stars and galaxies with some confidence.

It is perhaps interesting to speculate not only on how the universe began, but also on its very nature. Why are there physical laws? If we say they were ordained by God, where did God come from? Each era of science allows us to penetrate a bit further into our past. It is often pointed out that there was not enough time since the earth developed for evolution to provide us with humanity. The arguments to explain this range from "well, God did it" to the many worlds interpretation - that there are millions of unseen universes like ours where life did not develop - we were just lucky! Time does strange things. A friend of mine failed his Cambridge PhD thesis exam because his examiners did not believe in continental drift. "There is not enough time," they said. Similarly, there is not enough time for humanity - but there are other explanations. The fact remains: we are here, so there must be an explanation for our presence, but perhaps one that we now cannot comprehend!

As we speculate on the nature of God, it cannot help but puzzle us why the nature of the universe is so tied up with mathematics. The group theory on which much of quantum theory depends was developed earlier mathematically in the nineteenth century. It came as a great surprise to Heisenberg to find this had already been done when he needed it to explain the experiments, which had just been performed. As time has gone on, more and more complex mathematics has been required to explain experiments. Various symmetries seem to be necessary to explain the workings of the "Standard Model" of particle theory, and string theory itself, with its numerous dimensions, is also mathematically very complex. Richard Feynman once said that some damn fool will come along and show that the whole thing is simple. Unfortunately, the opposite seems to be true.

So that is how the universe began - but how will it end? At one time it was thought that gravity would slow the expansion of the universe, and pull it back in. Recently however, observations of distant type 1a supernovae showed that the rate of expansion is increasing. This acceleration, sometimes called the "big split", means that ultimately the universe will tear itself apart, stars will explode, and even molecules, atoms, and nuclei will be disintegrated. To bring this about a new entity called "dark energy" is postulated, which unlike gravity that draws matter together, instead forces it apart. As time evolves, ultimately this dark energy dominates still further.

This gives an overview of the universe - but of what is it constructed? The question the ancients tackled was: is it uniform or discrete? In other words, if you take a knife, and cut something in half, could you keep on doing this forever? Or would you reach a point where you found the universe to be composed of lumps, like a bag of marbles, rather than being uniform, like cheese for example. Lack of evidence rendered this problem unanswerable until fairly recently, and one would have said that the universe was composed of particles - the electron having been discovered in 1897 and subsequently, more and more particles. However it was less the particles themselves, and more the quantum theory, discovered almost simultaneously, which was important. About the same time, Einstein's theory of relativity, both special and general, replaced Newton's theory of gravity, and we were left with a completely different picture of the universe. More changes in this picture occur from time to time. The most recent picture invokes "fields" as the most fundamental quantity. Such fields fill all of space, giving rise to singularities that we identify as particles. The nature of these fields varies. The simplest fields we encounter are in electrostatics, where they are products of an inverse square law. The particles that such a field generates are called photons, which have no rest mass, and electrons, which do. Recently it has become clear that symmetries of various kinds govern the universe. We are all familiar with mirror symmetry - our hands are mirror symmetrical, left and right, but similar symmetries can be expanded to cover all the different particles of which the universe is composed. The "Standard Model" of the Universe conjures up the "eightfold way" with the recently discovered Higgs Boson generating the collection of particles.

The universe started with fundamental particles at a very high temperature, full of these things cooling off. After the universe had expanded enough, nuclei and atoms condensed - then the universe spread out, and galaxies and stars formed - together with molecules. The molecules were of all kinds, but the organic molecules – carbon-based but with hydrogen, oxygen, nitrogen, etc. included, proved capable of building themselves into strange complex units. Ultimately, some of these could duplicate and presto, we had life. This duplication process, together with evolution led us on so now we can communicate knowledge to one another - but ultimately the universe will explode into the "big split." Will that be the end? We don't know!

REPLY BY CHARLIE

I, of course, accept all of the observations that Ron has made concerning what science tells us about the origin and nature of the universe. His comments were very enlightening. However my perspective causes me to give totally different replies to the two questions being posed.

When a Christian considers the question: "Where did we as a community come from, and where will we go?" he thinks in terms of a sequence of events spanning many thousands of years. He thinks of God creating the world from nothing, and then creating man with an immortal soul. He recalls the fall from grace by Adam and Eve and the entrance of original sin into the world. Almost four thousand years ago came Abraham, Isaac, Jacob and the twelve tribes of Israel, and then came Moses, and the conquest of the Promised Land. Eventually David, followed by Solomon, ruled. Then came the conquests and exile. During the exile Buddha and Confucius made their appearances in the world. Then at the beginning of the first millennium Our Redeemer Jesus Christ came to Earth, preached for three years, was crucified, rose from the dead, ascended into Heaven, sent the Holy Spirit, and the Christian Church was founded.

The Church spread rapidly, survived many persecutions for 300 years, then became tolerated, and finally dominant despite many flourishing heresies. Eastern Orthodoxy went into schism in 1054. Then in the 16th century Martin Luther and John Calvin split Christianity into several Protestant denominations competing with Catholicism, which meanwhile had reformed itself at the Council of Trent (1545-1563). In the 20th century Pentecostalism arose to further split Christianity. At the present time Christianity is in competition with Islam for hegemony in the world. Over half of the people now alive profess one or the other of these two monotheistic Abrahamic faiths, as the following Table I indicates.

Table I. Religion population data.

<u>Worldwide Christianity</u>

Catholic:	1,100 Million	50%
Orthodox	250 "	11.5%
Protestant	460 "	21%

Pentecostal	390	"	17.5%
Anglicans	80	"	
Baptists	90	"	
Lutherans	75	"	
Methodists	75	"	
Presbyterians	70	"	

Worldwide Religions

Christians	2,200 Million		32%
Islam	1,700	"	25%
Hindus	1,100	"	16%
Buddhists	500	"	7%
Chinese Rel.	500	"	7%
Bahai Faith	9	"	0.01 %
Jews	14	"	0.02 %
Unaffiliated	800	"	12 %

The Secularist population, which is included under the category Unaffiliated, is not known, but is probably far in excess of 100 million. These data are only approximate as different demographers report diverse values.

The two paragraphs preceding Table I provide a typical Christian response to the first part of the above question: "Where did we come from?" The second part of the question: "Where will we go?" is perhaps best answered by a quotation from the end of the Nicene Creed (AD 325 and 381) concerning Jesus: "He will come again in glory to judge the living and the dead, and His Kingdom will have no end. We look for the resurrection of the dead and the life of the world to come." I personally reject all occasional predictions of an immanent ending of the world with a rapture (1 Thess. 4: 17).

When a Christian considers the related question: "Where did we as individuals come from, and where will we go?" the reply to the old Baltimore Catechism question: "Why did God make you?" comes to mind:

> God made me to know Him, to love Him, and to serve Him in this world so that I may be happy through Him in this life, and, after death, with Him forever in Heaven.

This reply tells it all! I have been and am now living my life with this itinerary ever in mind,

Chapter Seven

Miracles

INITIAL COMMENTS BY CHARLIE

Since its inception two thousand years ago Christianity has been a religion associated with reports of scientifically inexplicable occurrences that are often referred to as miracles. It is time for impartial scientists and other academics to examine this evidence and attempt to explain it. If some of these various events can be confirmed as scientifically inexplicable or miraculous it would provide strong evidenced that: (a) God exists, (b) God interacts with mankind, and (c) Christianity is the true religion of God. Unfortunately, these probable consequences make it unlikely that well-known and reputable scientists will be willing to evaluate this readily available evidence for God. Most scientists take pride in how their colleagues work so hard to explain empirical data, especially when the data seem to conflict with currently accepted scientific theories and viewpoints. Unfortunately, there is a strong prejudice within the scientific community against entertaining the possibility that there might be a spiritual aspect to nature. This makes it incumbent on Christian leaders to spread the word of the existence of these easily verifiable and scientifically inexplicable data. In this article we will review many of the data that exist, and we will urge their examination and critique by scientists in the interest of fairness. Scientists consider every aspect of nature to be within their domain, and we ask them to prove this. We quote a word of scripture for them (Mt: 14, 27): "Be not afraid" to investigate **all** of nature, that is **the totality of nature**.

45

If and when scientists become more willing to evaluate the evidence for these miracles they will undoubtedly try to provide materialistic explanations for all of them. We would hope, however, that if and when the evidence for miracles is most reasonably explained by appealing to supernatural factors then the scientists will be sufficiently broad minded and impartial to take this into account. I as a professional physicist would expect this objectivity and courtesy from my scientific colleagues.

THE INCORRUPTIBLES

The first set of experimental data that constitute evidence for miracles of divine origin are the bodies of over 80 saintly individuals which remained preserved without decay for many years after their death[1.] In many cases the bodies had not been embalmed. More specifically there are records of over 60 bodies remaining preserved for more than 100 years, 26 of them having been incorrupt for in excess of 500 years. At the present time over two-dozen shrines around the world have either in storage or on display the incorrupt bodies of saintly individuals. For example, the body of St. Agatha, who was martyred in 251 AD, is now preserved in several reliquaries. Her arms and legs are dried and dark, but still incorrupt. In the cases of some, the body was found preserved at the first exhumation, and decayed at a subsequent one, and in other cases it remained incorrupt though several successive exhumations. Exhumations often took place when the individual was being considered for sainthood, or when his or her remains were being moved to new location. In some cases only part of the body remains incorrupt, such as the heart of St. Jane Frances de Chantal, (d. 1641), and that of St. Jean-Baptiste Vianney, the Curé of Ars (d. 1859). There have been miracles associated with the shrines of some of the incorrupt bodies, and in a few cases the bodies have stigmata imprinted on them. It would be appropriate and informative for scientists to now examine and evaluate, utilizing state of the art instrumentation, as many of the presently available uncorrupt bodies as they can. The bodies of dead people inevitably decompose with time, and when this decay is delayed for several decades or for several centuries it is a truly inexplicable occurrence, patently in the category of a genuine miracle. It is difficult to explain many of these occurrences without invoking the intervention of the Lord acting in a miraculous manner.

HEALINGS OF DISEASES

The miraculous preservation of the incorrupt bodies that were just discussed is not widely known outside of Roman Catholic circles, but the opposite is the case with respect to the miraculous healings that have taken place at the shrine of Lourdes in France[2, 3]. Many unexplained and authenticated healings of bodily injuries and infirmities have been recorded at shrines such as this. The Lourdes Medical Bureau was established at the Shrine to make sure that every cure is properly examined, to verify its authenticity, and thereby preserve the shrine from false claims of miracles. This Bureau is completely under the supervision of medical authorities, with no involvement of church officials. For a cure to be accepted as medically inexplicable it must satisfy several conditions: 1) the original diagnosis must be verified and confirmed, 2) the ailment must be organic (having no psychosomatic aspect), be grave, and be judged as incurable, 3) the cure must be instantaneous, complete, and permanent, and 4) it must occur associated with a visit to Lourdes.

If a disabled pilgrim comes to Lourdes, he or she is statistically very unlikely to be cured. Of the 80,000 pilgrims who come every year about 35 claim cures, but the medical bureau usually only accepts three to five of these claims as meriting a more thorough investigation. Very often none of them are judged as medically inexplicable. Thus a truly miraculous cure is very unlikely. Anyone who is judged cured is urged to return a year later to confirm that the cure is permanent. With all these precautions in place it seems scientifically reasonable to accept the medically inexplicable cures as arising from interventions of God in the lives of human beings.

GUADALUPE AND THE TILMA

An important miracle took place on December 9, 1531 near the shrine of Guadalupe in Mexico City where there is currently on display the tilma (cloak or poncho) of Juan Diego on which was imprinted an image of the Virgin Mary[4]. The tilma is a thin cloth made of cactus fibers that under normal circumstances would have decayed in less than 40 years, but has now survived still soft to the touch and intact after over five and a half centuries[3]. The fabric and the imprinted image have undergone several technical studies since 1751 that confirm that it is a genuine relic of the Nahuatl (native Indian) culture dating from the early 16th century. The image on the tilma is not paint, and has no natural explanation. Ophthalmologists report an image in the eyes of the imprinted Virgin (Samson-Purkinje Effect). There appears to be a definite involvement of the supernatural here. What other reasonable or adequate explanation is there for the events that took place in Mexico at the imprinting in the year 1531?

MIRACLE OF THE SUN AT FATIMA 1917

The miracle of the Sun was associated with a lady, who later identified herself as the Virgin Mary, who appeared in Fatima, Portugal[2] to three young children Lucia, Francisco, and Jacinta, aged 10, 8 and 7, respectively, on the 13th day of May through October, 1917. On July 13th she proclaimed: "In October . . . I will perform a miracle for all to see and believe." Then on October 13th in the presence of many thousands of assembled people the sun was observed to "dance in the sky," to spin like a pinwheel, and to rapidly dry everyone's rain soaked clothes. Local and out of town newspapers published sensational reports of the event which had no natural explanation. Many of the onlookers knew that the miracle had been predicted three months earlier. With so many eyewitnesses present, it should be acknowledged by all as a genuine miracle. The revelations and predictions made to the three young children also deserve to be evaluated anew.

EUCHARISTIC MIRACLES.

Throughout the centuries of the second millennium there have been many miracles associated with hosts of bread and/or wine consecrated during Mass[5, 6] (celebrations of the Lord's Supper). The earliest recorded miracle took place about the year 700 when a priest-monk who was celebrating Mass doubted that the bread and wine would become the body and blood of the Lord. He was astonished when at the point of consecration, the host turned into flesh, and the wine became blood. He informed the congregation, and they came up to the altar to witness the miracle. After the Mass the flesh remained intact, but the blood congealed into five pellets. When the pellets were weighed all five of them together had the same weight as any one of them individually. This weight anomaly was confirmed on several occasions.

The book by Cruz[5] records 14 cases in which the sacred host and /or blood remains preserved today, and 16 cases in which it had been preserved for many years but remains so no longer. There are some instances in which what are preserved is bloodstains on a corporal or purificator cloth. In several instances the blood had spurted out of the consecrated host and stained the cloth. In addition, there have been some recorded miracles associated with the preserved consecrated hosts. In many cases the preserved hosts and blood have been examined technically and their status authenticated by qualified experts. Many thousands of pilgrims have visited the shrines where the evidences of the Eucharistic miracles are located, and many of them are convinced of their authenticity. Perhaps the most important thing is that they constitute experimental data that defy materialistic explanations, and hence provide verifiable proofs that the Lord God is watching over His people. More specifically these miracles provide experimental evidence in support of the claim that when the priest pronounces the words of consecration "this is my body" and "this is the cup of my blood" an actual transformation can and does take place. As we mentioned above, on several occasions the bread and wine were observed to actually transform into flesh and blood.

STIGMATA

Further evidence for miracles taking place during modern times comes from Stigmatists, that is, from individuals endowed with the stigmata or the imprinting of the wounds of the Lord's passion and crucifixion on the flesh of their bodies[7-9]. Many believe that St. Paul was the first stigmatist since he says in Gal. 6:17 "I bear on my body the marks of Jesus." Well over a thousand years were to pass before Francis of Assisi was endowed with the stigmata on September 14, 1224. After that he spent the remaining two years of his life away from the day-to-day management of his Franciscan order, losing himself in the Crucified Christ. He had, unknowingly, set the Church in a new direction. Several women saints subsequently acquired stigmata: Catherine of Siena (d. 1380), Rita of Casia (d. 1457), Osanna of Mantua (d.1505) in Italy, then Rose of Lima (d. 1617) in Peru. There have been a number of recent stigmatists such as Anne Catherine Emmerich (d. 1824), Sister Faustina Kowalaska (d. 1938), Theresa Neumann (d. 1962), and Padre Pio of Pietrelcina (d. 1968), the only priest known to have been favored with the stigmata.

Most stigmatists belonged to communities within which their condition was common knowledge, and had been observed by many. Ordinarily each had the five traditional wounds of Jesus, two imprinted on their hands, two on their feet, and one on their side. They also had to endure the pain that accompanied these wounds. In addition, some had the additional stigma of a crown of thorns wounds on their head (stigma is the singular of the plural word stigmata). The hand wound was usually in the center of the palm, which is where it appears in almost all artwork, even though at the actual crucifixion it was almost certainly through the wrist where the nail is capable of supporting the weight of a crucified man. Over the centuries the great majority of stigmatists have been Roman Catholics, but in recent years one was a Baptist, one belonged to a small Celtic church, and at least three were Anglicans[8].

MIRACULOUS FASTING

Further support for the intervention of the Lord in the affairs of mankind comes from the claim that a number of saints have subsisted on little or no food for many months, or even many years, with no apparent damage to their brain or to their body, a phenomenon called inedia. A number of such individuals ingested only the Eucharist during the duration of their inedia. Three examples of such individuals are the stigmatists Catherine of Siena, Anne Catherine Emmerich, and Theresa Neumann. Catherine of Siena subsisted for years only on the Eucharist, and she also had a body that remained incorrupt after she died, The various cases of recorded inedia would, without doubt, be extremely difficult to authenticate to the satisfaction of skeptical scientists.

SHROUD OF TURIN

The Shroud of Turin is an ancient linen burial cloth that has inscribed on it the negative image of a crucified man[10-12]. It is stored at the Cathedral of St. John the Baptist in Turin, Italy, where it is occasionally on display for the public, perhaps several times a century. Prior to the carbon-14 dating to the year 1325 and the range of dates (1292 - 1358) some historians had associated the Shroud with an indistinct image of a man's head (i.e. the head of Jesus) located in the city of Edessa, Asia Minor, in the year 544 AD. This image was brought to Constantinople in 944 but disappeared after the Crusaders sacked the city in 1204. Since the 6th century portraits of Christ have exhibited features resembling those on the Shroud, which probably also resembled the Edessa image. The Shroud itself appeared in Lirey, France in the year 1357, and its whereabouts have been well documented since then. Several species of pollen removed from the Shroud are indigenous to Asia Minor and Palestine.

The image itself is a thin layer on the surface of the herringbone linen fibers; hence, it cannot be paint. Scientists have made extensive studies of the image, and are unable to identify its origin, or to duplicate it. Negative images were unknown until the development of photography during the 19th century, so a mediaeval craftsman could never have produced the Shroud image. The Shroud pattern exhibits three-dimensional imaging features not possible from a fabricated image. Its nature and its origin are a mystery to scientists. The extensive scientific tests carried out on the Shroud exemplify what could and should be done to try and authenticate or disprove the other experimental data of alleged miracles that we have been discussing.

CANONIZATION MIRACLES

When the Catholic Church pronounces a deceased person as a Blessed and subsequently as a Saint, it requires a miracle for the first step in the process, and two miracles for the second and final step. Pope John Paul II canonized 480 saints, more than all previous popes since the year 1588, which corresponds to well over 1,500 miracles that have been performed and documented. Most of these were healings of diseases, that is cures that were complete, instantaneous, lasting, and with no natural explanation. Thus there are records of more than 1,500 miracles that could be investigated and either authenticated or discredited by scientists.

We have catalogued several varieties of events and associated experimental data that have been classified as miraculous by countless Christians, and as inexplicable by some scientists. When confronted with these novel data the judgment rendered by scientists is ordinarily not "miraculous" but rather "scientifically inexplicable." Nevertheless, the knowledge of these events suggests the reality of the intervention of God in the world, and the validity of the religion of Christianity. As a physicist I challenge qualified and impartial scientific colleagues to examine and objectively evaluate the evidence detailed in this article.

RESPONSE BY RON

The thoughtful article on miracles requires some critical discussion by a skeptic. Firstly, the definition of a miracle as a "scientifically inexplicable occurrence." Yet to my mind, a universe governed by scientific laws is a miracle in itself. It has often been pointed out that if the values of scientific constants, such as the speed of light, were to change in the slightest degree, life on this earth would be impossible. This has lead to the development of the "anthropic principle". The solution to the problem lies in the concept that there are millions of invisible universes not too dissimilar from ours, but sufficiently different so life could not exist. Of course, we are on the only one where everything is just right. We would never know about the others. We happen to exist at just the right time. We could not have survived on earth had we been here even 10% before or later than the present era. We were lucky -unless you believe someone or something put us here. There is, however, no proof of that.

Back to the odd occurrences we call miracles. For the most part, most of these events date back from before the scientific era. Two things then emerge. Firstly, it was easier to accept such events as an "act of God". So much so it has even found its way into our legal terminology. With a concept so deeply embedded in the public mentality, it is difficult to be objective. Secondly, people were a little less observant in those days. Nevertheless, there were undoubtedly things that went on which were difficult to explain. However, it may be worthwhile to give examples, which today have a simple explanation. Walking through a dark forest at night, luminous ghosts were observed on the trees. These ghosts vanished as soon as you looked at them. Superficially, this would seem difficult to explain scientifically, but easy on a supernatural basis. Yet recently a simple explanation occurred. The retina of the eye is such that the fovea, which is in the center where you look, has the highest definition - vision is sharp there. However, it is not very sensitive. The peripheral vision cells are much more sensitive. Hence, in walking through a dark forest, these sensitive cells respond to the glowing fungus on trees out of the corner of the eye - yet when you look directly at these glowing "ghosts", they vanish, because their image falls on the less sensitive fovea, which is much less responsive. Hence something originally thought supernatural proves to have a simple explanation.

Referring to Poole's data on the preserved bodies of saintly individuals, my first thought would be, who benefits by their preservation? Apart from the individuals who run the mausoleum, presumably only people wanting to reverence the saint. This was, of course, the point of difference between some Christian faiths, which believe there should be no graven images around - not even candlesticks on the altar. The problem of authenticity also arises. Can one be sure that a body a thousand years old is the original? Yet thousands of people come to worship at such shrines. It would seem to be rather sad if this was not the original. Nevertheless, it would give people a focus for worship.

The requirements for beatification are considerable. There are various levels to go through. However, there is no doubt that the performance of a miracle presents the greatest hurdle. Medical miracles can present the greatest uncertainty. After all, there are many patients who get better with no clear reason why, even in the absence of miracles.

Consider the specific case of Guadalupe and Juan Diego, who was not canonized until 2002 as the first indigenous American saint. He saw an apparition of the Virgin Mary in

1531. A lot can happen between, and one wonders how much belief to put in reports from that far back. Physical evidence is required unless the evidence of bystanders is to be believed.

The miracle of Fatima became well publicized. In this case, the Virgin Mary appeared to three children. Children do not make good witnesses, so it is difficult to accept that they had in fact seen the Virgin, although they were very definite about what had occurred. What is difficult to explain is the peculiar vision of the sun "dancing in the sky" seen by many thousands of people at the time and place where one of the children, Lucia, predicted. A possible explanation has been put forward by Professor Auguste Meessen of the Catholic University of Leuven, who postulated that staring at the sun affects the retina, causing partial blindness and peculiar visual effects such as those described. Similar events occurred at Herolsbach, Germany in 1949. Lucia went on to have many more such visions before dying at the advanced age of 97.

Other evidence for miracles quoted are stigmata. These are the imprints thought to simulate the wounds Christ suffered whilst on the cross. These generally consist of two wounds through the palms of the hands, two through the feet and one in the side. The trouble with this is that, as Poole suggests, modern evidence implies the wounds occurred not through the hands but the wrists. The reason is that, for the body to be supported on the cross, it is necessary for the nails to go through the wrists. Otherwise, the body would tear off. Similarly, the legs might be bent, and the nails put through much higher up than the feet for the same reason. However even this is uncertain, and experiments have been performed to show that the body could be supported by nails through the hands, provided the arms were not spread at a suitable angle. The actual nature of the stigmata also varies. In some cases, it is actual wounds, and in others merely imprints. St. Francis was ostensibly the first stigmatist, and there has been much speculation on the physical cause for the stigmata. St Francis suffered from numerous physical ailments, at least one of which could have led to the marks, and also the bleeding. In some respects, Los Penetentes of New Mexico have similarities to stigmatists. These individuals have themselves deliberately crucified at Easter. This procedure is not sanctioned by the Catholic Church. It would appear however that they recover after the event.

Miraculous fasting is also said to have occurred specifically with individuals surviving merely on the host provided at Eucharist (communion). There is firm evidence for this, although how much and how often the host was consumed is not clear. It takes very little food to keep an elderly woman alive.

Much attention has been paid to the so-called "Shroud of Turin", which has been followed since 1357. The suggestion that the image on the shroud was that of Christ has been firmly negated by radioactive dating of threads taken from the shroud, although it makes a nice tale, the evidence being that the shroud does date back to the fourteenth century.

Of the at least 1500 miracles authenticated by the Catholic Church, most were medical cures. It is very difficult to authenticate these cures, and furthermore there are many cures which occur spontaneously without spiritual help, and which, for the most part, are not recorded as such. Our medical knowledge is still so primitive; it is hard to understand what has occurred, in most instances. It follows that genuine scientists are very skeptical of miraculous cures. Too often it has been found that mock physicians have falsified their results for their own purposes. It is for this reason the Catholic Church is very cautious about canonizing. Nevertheless, a true skeptic tends to be suspicious, with the notorious findings concerning spiritualists, who seek to contact the dead.

Perhaps the universe is like a well-built car. It will run perfectly for a long while, but even the best-built car will have an occasional glitch that needs fixing. Is this occasional glitch like a miracle? Something that violates the rules, and needs seeing to? The trouble with this analogy is that such glitches are random, whereas ostensibly miracles occur when necessary. Since our knowledge of the physics of the universe is changing day by day, perhaps our views about God and miracles will also change. We can no longer have God throw thunderbolts, but a God who created the symmetry group SU3 for the eightfold way and the Standard Model for particle physics? That takes some thinking about.

In conclusion, scientists, although very skeptical, hesitate to rule out miraculous events, unless they have definite physical evidence. In most instances only time and new physical tools will make the decision. For example, DNA tests on the body will help determine its origin, the DNA from an American Indian being so different from a westerner.

Chapter Eight

The God of the Gaps

INITIAL COMMENTS BY RON

Primitive cultures believed that all physical phenomena were the product of action by the gods. So if you were struck by lightning it occurred because the gods were upset with you, presumably because of something you had done which angered them. Modern knowledge of the physics of thunderstorms has led to the predictions of meteorology, and our belief of gods as a fundamental generator of lightning has vanished. The same has gone on for a vast number of other problems, all of which have had simple (sometimes not so simple) physical solutions. This has led to a concept called "God of the gaps".

This suggests that if there is something we cannot explain, we attribute it to God- a God arising because of our lack of knowledge. The interesting thing is, that as our knowledge of previously inexplicable phenomena improves, it merely leads to even more sophisticated inexplicable phenomena. At the end of the nineteenth century, Lord Kelvin, a famous physicist, advised a student not to go into physics, because it was already all known. Then along came quantum mechanics to reveal to us completely new, inexplicable phenomena. Now we find that about 75% of the universe is composed of dark energy and we have not the foggiest idea what it is, plus a good 20% of dark matter, and we also have not a vague idea what that might be, with only 5% or so composed of ordinary matter which we fully understand. That leaves a lot to God. Thus we do not have to look very far to reach a point where we do not understand what is going on.

Let us just look at the constants of physics. Why is the velocity of light a constant? Was it just by good luck that we landed in this universe, as the anthropic principle suggests? So far every so-called "theory of everything" has merely led to even deeper unknowns. When I was a kid, it was thought that the nucleus with the electron buzzing round it was the ultimate solution for everything, but then along came quarks and the multitude of unstable fundamental particles, and now we have the eightfold way, string theory, dark matter and dark energy. It doesn't look as if this is the end, either. At least it makes life, as well as physics, interesting.

Can we predict what the gaps are in our knowledge? Well, starting at the beginning, there is the big bang. But what came before the big bang? Perhaps there was nothing - maybe time did not exist yet - now there is an almighty gap for a start. That immediately leads to - where will it end? Right now it looks as though the universe will just continue to blow apart - forever. At present there is an unsatisfactory ending if ever there was one. It would be nice if the universe started to collapse, then to commence a cycle again, but there is no evidence of that. It follows that nice, simple solutions are unlikely to be the answer. The universe is a puzzle of the mightiest degree. Yet it is a puzzle, and not the chaos that might have been.

There has been a lot of discussion about a "theory of everything". Yet the evidence has shown this is a most unlikely proposition. Instead, our knowledge resembles more a jigsaw puzzle. As we continue to work in physics, the puzzle begins to fill out, from the center, but we do not anticipate that it will be completed, with a nice edge. Instead, as one section is completed, it merely leads to another farther out and so on, with each part becoming more and more involved. There seems to be no evidence that we are approaching completion of the puzzle, since inevitably it wanders to new and different unexpected directions.

REPLY BY CHARLIE

In his above "God of the Gaps" essay Ron mentioned that physicists find 95% of the physical universe inexplicable, namely the parts that consist of dark energy (75%) and dark matter (20%). He also pointed out that this unintelligible portion is often attributed to a so-called "God of the Gaps." As a firmly believing Christian I reject the concept of a god of the gaps, since my belief is in the Christian triune God who is more properly called a "God of the Spirit." This God is a Trinity of three divine persons called the Father, the Son and the Holy Spirit who have eternal inter-relationships of love with each other. This God created the world and sustains it in existence. The Son, Jesus Christ, the second person of the Trinity, assumed a human nature in addition to his divine nature, and spent 33 years on earth. He suffered crucifixion to atone for the sins of mankind, then rose from the dead and inspired his Apostles and other disciples to found His Church to which, I belong. At the end of the Gospel of Matthew (28: 19) Jesus commissioned his disciples: "Go, therefore, and make disciples of all nations," a task which, two thousand years later, is still in progress with no apparent delays or "gaps."

Perhaps, sometime, Ron and I should eventually debate the possibility of, the existence of, and the purpose of, a God!

Chapter Nine

The Soul

INITIAL COMMENTS BY CHARLIE

The soul is the spiritual component of a person. In Aristotelian or Thomistic matter & form terminology, the soul is the form and the material body is the matter of a human being. The soul will survive forever after death either eternally rewarded for a life righteously lived or ended in genuine sorrow for the sins of the past, or condemned to suffer eternally in hell for a non-repented sinful life. The soul is spiritual - endowed with an intellect and a will.

Evidence for the existence of a human soul comes from reports of near-death experiences (NDEs) and out-of-body experiences. A near death experience can occur, e.g., when falling from a great height, near drowning, and undergoing a surgical operation. For example, there are cases in which an unconscious person undergoing a surgical operation has his heart stop for a short time, and he is then revived. During the operation he has the experience of being out of his body looking down on the operation from above. Afterward he recounts details of the procedure to the physicians and nurses, and they are amazed at this. The only reasonable explanation is that the soul had temporarily left his body. There are several characteristics that accompany many NDEs, such as experiencing separation from the body, feeling peace and contentment, entering darkness, and seeing and sometimes entering a bright light. A Gallup poll reports that approximately eight million Americans claim to have had a near-death experience. The International Association of Near

Death Studies gathers evidence for, and collects reports of NDEs.

REPLY BY RON

What is the "soul"? Most religions split our existence into physical and spiritual. The soul represents the spiritual. However, at that point there are a semi-infinite number of concepts defining the soul, and what happens to it after death. If we were to categorize these, clearly the first category are those who don't believe we have a soul, and therefore what happens after death is of no interest. This does not mean we have no influence after death. We live on, physically, through our progeny. To see this, we have merely to look at our friends, neighbors, or important people. Take the Roosevelts for example. Here we have a whole family of politicians. Since they are always appearing in the press, their heritage is obvious. They have political souls. Or take actors. The families of actors are again well known. The Barrymores, and the Lupino family all have their roots in the acting profession. Appearance is also inherited. There is the famous chin of the Hapsburgs (called "prognathism") and, in fact we can trace back our ancestry to the wilds of Africa via our DNA. So does our DNA determine our soul? This leads to the fundamental question, do animals have souls? Most people would agree that the fly crawling up the window has no soul, but many dog owners would contend that their Fido has a soul, and would have him buried with a suitable tombstone. Perhaps he has a dog soul - with a great Dane as super-god! It follows that communication and intelligence for humanity may have much to do with our belief in a soul. The slaves brought over from Africa were thought to be soul-less, partly because of lack of communication with their owners (and it was more ethical and profitable if they were soul less!) Our present day ability to communicate both verbally and visually over the whole earth has led to the ability to disseminate information in ways not previously possible. Perhaps this will lead to a joint soul for all mankind - or at least a small branch of it.

Our concept of the soul is contingent on the belief that we can divide our existence into two parts - the concrete and the spiritual. There is no concrete evidence for the spiritual part and the spiritual part generally ignores the concrete. Nevertheless, mankind has attributed all sorts of phenomena to the soul, and it pervades virtually all religions. So how can such an embedded belief not be true? Perhaps it is an inherent part of our brains - whether it exists or not, our brains make us believe it so. It has been suggested that our observed existence may be merely a figment of our imaginations. So you exist merely through my imagination, as does the rest of the universe. In fact, such bizarre concepts can be neither proved not disproved.

The concept of a soul predates Greek and Roman times, but the advent of computers has led to a different concept. Can computers have a soul? After all, in many respects they can think better than we do! There is Alan Turing's test. If you communicate with a real human and a computer, how can you tell which is which?

Most religions believe in a soul, Perhaps UUs differ in that they can make a choice.

Christians believe in a soul as distinct from yet connected with the body, and when we die this soul can either go to heaven or hell (after God's judgment), or in some cases something between called limbo. The assistance of Jesus Christ intercedes in this judgment process, particularly when it comes to babies and people with mental problems. Then there is purgatory where you go to have your soul purged; i.e. in Catholic belief, it is a temporary residence for the soul in preparation for heaven. The existence of a soul in the unborn plays a part in the discussion of the ethics of abortion. In earlier eras, it was believed that the entry of the soul was connected with "quickening" when the mother first felt the fetus move, and realized something was alive inside her.

Judaism predates Christianity by many centuries, so its basic construction is more primitive, although it is past the belief in sentient stones and such. Modern Hebrews believe the soul is given by God to a person at his first breath as mentioned in Genesis. Hence the rabbinical interpretation that embryos do not have souls. The soul returns to God after death. The Kabbalah separates the soul into five elements.

Most Protestant beliefs in the soul are similar to Catholic -but others do differ; Lutherans, for example, believing that after death the soul sleeps until the resurrection of the dead.

Hindus have a complex view of what is meant by the soul. The Sanskrit word "aatma" is often used which covers a wide range of meaning - "self" is often used, but with a more eternal meaning, part of the "immensity" or supreme self of the universe. Hence, whereas Christianity separates God and man, Hinduism suggests man is part of God, and this extends to his soul.

In the Quran, Islam teaches that the soul is immortal and eternal, and will later be judged.

Sikhs believe the soul (aatma) to be a part of God, but there is wide divergence of views as to what happens after death.

It will be seen that, whereas most religions posit that everyone has a soul, they differ widely on what this means. The scientific point of view is exemplified by Francis Crick in his book "The Astonishing Hypothesis" subtitled "The scientific search for the soul". Crick believed you could learn everything about the human soul by studying the workings of the brain. So neuroscience will ultimately explain the soul. However others believe one cannot explain the non-substantial soul with the substantial brain.

Chapter Ten

The Trinity

INITIAL COMMENTS BY CHARLIE

I am a Christian scientist in the sense that I am a Catholic physicist, and as such one of my main interests as a physicist is the structure that exists in the world. I discuss this in my 22 published books on Superconductivity, Nanotechnology, and other topics. For example, many solids are made up of small molecules, each molecule is an array of smaller atoms, and each atom consists of an even smaller nucleus surrounded by a cloud of electrons. The structure runs even deeper since each nucleus is formed from protons and neutrons, which in turn consist of quarks. The biological realm also has structure, with animal bodies formed from organs, which in turn consist of tissues constructed from tinier cells, each with a complex subcellular structure, and so on. In addition, the vast cosmos that surrounds us in outer space also exhibits structure associated with its content of between ten- and a hundred-billion galaxies, each of which contains, on the average, between ten- and a hundred-billion stars plus many planets and other ingredients. Thus the presence of structure seems to be a characteristic feature of the entire Universe!

As a Christian scientist, I of course, not only believe in God, but in addition I consider Jesus Christ as my divine Lord and Savior. The physicist in me, and the accompanying curiosity, prompt me to pose the following two questions:

Is there structure in God?

And if so, what is its nature?

The Christian belief, of course, is that there is a threefold or triune variety of structure, with the one and only God consisting of three divine persons, called the Father, the Son, and the Holy Spirit. In antiquity there were many polytheistic religions. Their structure involved interpersonal relations among their several gods. The ancient Roman and Greek religions had, respectively, Jupiter and Zeus, as the chief, but certainly not a supreme, type of god. Christianity is the only monotheistic religion with structure in its God, something that attracts my attention as a Christian Scientist. My instincts lead me to try to elucidate, and hopefully to possibly comprehend the significance of this structure. Several recent books have appeared on this subject.

We are all familiar with some of the classical New Testament verses that are suggestive of the Trinity. At the baptism of Jesus, "There came a voice from heaven: Thou art my beloved Son; in thee I am well pleased" (Mark 1:11). The Gospel of Matthew ends (28:19) with the commission: "Go, therefore, and make disciples of all nations, baptizing them in the name of the Father, and of the Son, and of the Holy Spirit." Just before His ascension Jesus said to the apostles, "You will receive power when the Holy Spirit comes upon you" (Acts 1:8). Then later at Pentecost we read (Acts 2: 3,4), "Then there appeared to them tongues as of fire, which parted and came to rest on each of them. And they were all filled with the Holy Spirit and began to speak in different tongues, as the Spirit enabled them to proclaim." There are the words of Jesus recorded in the Gospel of John (14: 16), "The advocate, the holy Spirit that the Father will send in my name - he will teach you everything." There are a number of other passages in scripture that provide support for the doctrine of the Trinity, and some of them will be alluded to later in this article.. During the first few centuries of Christianity there were disputes in the Church about the status of Jesus and the nature of God. To settle these disputes Ecumenical Councils were convened[11], and the first four were held at Nicaea (325 AD), Constantinople (381), Ephesus (431), and Chalcedon (451). These councils decreed that there are three persons in God called the Father, the Son, and the Holy Spirit. They also decided that Jesus Christ possesses both a divine nature and a human nature. The episcopal delegates at the councils found it necessary to utilize non-biblical, philosophical terminology during their deliberations. For example, nature refers to the essence of a being, that by which it is what it is, and a person is an individual substance of a rational nature, where a substance is something that exists through itself or in itself, and not in another.

Historically there have been two perspectives, or points of view, concerning how to think about the Trinity. The more fundamental perspective, called the Immanent Trinity, concerns the Divine Persons with respect to one another. The other perspective, called the Economic Trinity, concerns how the Divine Persons relate to the world and to salvation history. A common economic viewpoint is, "The Father creates, the Son redeems, and the Spirit sanctifies." Prior to Vatican II theological treatises, such as that of Adolphe Tanquery[13], had separate sections on *De Deo Uno* and *De Deo Trino*. Karl Rahner[9] is well known for proposing the famous so-called *Rahner Axiom*: "The 'economic' Trinity is the 'immanent' Trinity, and vice versa. I do not understand the subtleties that underlie this axiom; so it is not very meaningful to me personally.

Concerning the Immanent Trinity Christians believe that the Son has a relation of origin, or of begetting, from the Father, technically called "filiation". The Son was begotten of the Father from all eternity, as the Nicene Creed says. Later the Nicene Creed was modified to say that the Holy Spirit "proceeds from the Father and the Son," an action technically called "spiration," which was also from all eternity. The Latin expression for "and from the Son" is *filioque*[10], and this brings on a short digression.

The usual Latin expression for "the father and the son" is "*pater et filius*" and there is also the shorter form of this "*pater filiusque.*" where the suffix "*que*" means "and". These are nominative cases. The expression "from the Father and the Son" makes use of ablative cases: "patre filioque" in the Creed. The original Creedal proclamations at Nicea (325) and Constantinople (381) omitted the *filioque.* It began being inserted into the Creed at Toledo Spain in the year 587 AD, and in succeeding years the practice gradually spread throughout the Western or Catholic branch of the first millennium Church. A motivation for the insertion was to help combat heresies. The Eastern, or Orthodox, branch of the first millennium Church always considered the insertion of *"filioque"* into the Creed as heretical, and they continue to preach that today. Unfortunately, the Ecumenical Councils of Lateran IV (1215) and Florence (1438-45) declared its insertion as a dogma. At the present time Catholics and Protestants acknowledge the double procession of the Holy Spirit when they recite the Creed, and the Orthodox insist on retaining the original single procession. The Catholic and Orthodox branches of the one true Church, among other concerns, in disagreement over the *filioque* issue, excommunicated each other and inaugurated the Great Schism in the year 1054, almost a thousand years ago. It is high time to make up and reconcile over the *filioque* situation. Most of our children and grandchildren will be alive to either bemoan or celebrate the Millennial Anniversary of the Schism in the soon to arrive year 2054!

Let us return to the discussion of the nature of the Trinity. The three Divine Persons experience internal relationships reciprocally in each other through a mutual indwelling, or interpenetration, called operations *ad intra,* or perichoresis. These relations help to define their personhoods. They also have operations *ad extra* called missions, or sendings, of Divine Persons to the material world or to the economy of salvation.   Rahner [9] claims that all *ad extra* operations or missions such as the creation of the world are carried out by all three persons acting together in unison with each other. The incarnation, birth, passion, crucifixion, and resurrection of Jesus would seem to be important exceptions to this general principle, casting doubt on the validity of the Rahner principle. There are some Old Testament texts that foreshadow the Trinity like Isaiah 6:3: "Holy, Holy, Holy, Lord God of Hosts" and 61:4 "The spirit of the Lord God is upon me." Sometimes in the New Testament the three Divine Persons are mentioned in close proximity, as in Luke 1:32, 35 where the angel Gabriel says to the Virgin Mary: "He shall be great, and shall be called the Son of the most High...The Holy Spirit shall come upon thee, and the power of the most High shall overshadow thee, and therefore the Holy which shall be born of thee shall be called the Son of God." At the Last Supper Jesus told His apostles that he was "going to the Father" and that He planned to ask the Father to send the Paraclete, the Spirit of truth (John 16:7-13). Most of the references in the bibliography[1-11] provide citations to New Testament passages where two, or occasionally all three, of the Divine Persons are mentioned together.

Of the first eleven books in the bibliography some were written by Catholics and others by Protestants. In reading these various books it was usually not easy to identify the theological background of the authors since they all had similar viewpoints on the various aspects of the Trinity doctrine. I consider it significant that believers from the various denominations have such similar approaches toward comprehending the nature of this teaching. When I read a book on another theological topic such as ecclesiology, grace and justification, or predestination, it is generally much easier to identify the background of the authors.

The widespread Pentecostalist movement that began at the Azusa Street Revival from 1906 to 1909 led in Los Angeles by W. J. Seymour is considered by many as a modern manifestation of the Holy Spirit in the world. It is characterized by Baptism of the Holy Ghost and glossalalia, or "speaking in tongues." Many of these Pentecostals have retained membership in their more traditional Christian denominations. A main common factor that bonds together various branches of Christianity is their jointly confessing worship of the Triune God, utilizing the words of the ancient, almost two-thousand year old, Nicene Creed[12].

The Christian doctrine of the Trinity is really only of particular interest to Christians. It provides them with a way of understanding how their Lord and Savior Jesus Christ can be understood as a divine person. My physicist friend Chris Edge observes that what we have said about the Trinity emphasizes the amazing reality that because the three persons are truly separate persons, although one in being, it enables the possibility that the second person of the Trinity could truly enter into the experiences, of suffering, and isolation that are characteristic of the human condition. In addition, our exposition provides unbelievers such as agnostics with an example of how God can possess structure like everything else in the universe.

From a more general perspective in Table I of Chapter 6 we take into account the demographics of religious belief in the world. We see from this table that a third of the people now present on earth are Christians so the doctrine of the Trinity is of interest to at least one out of every three of the people who are living today. Another third of the population are Buddhists, Hindus, members of Chinese religions or are unaffiliated so they have no concept of a personal God, or of a Trinity, A remaining quarter of humanity, namely Baha'is, Jews and Moslems, have a firm belief in a Father type of God called Yahweh or Allah, and a firm rejection of the concept of a Trinity or of any structure in God. Nevertheless, it is encouraging to realize that one- third of humanity reveres Jesus Christ, the second person of the Blessed Trinity, and hopefully this proportion will increase in time.

It is also interesting to point out what Mitch Stokes tells us in his recent biography of Isaac Newton[13] who spent a great deal of time during his later years writing about theology. Newton struggled to understand the Trinity while preparing for ordination to the Anglican priesthood, changing his position on this topic several times during this struggle. His notes on the Trinity became public only after his death. In her 2012 book *Trinity in Relation* Gloria Schaab expressed the viewpoint that relationships are all there is to reality.

We saw above how from the viewpoint of the immanent or *ad intra* Trinity the three Divine Persons experience internal relationships reciprocally to each other through a mutual indwelling, or interpenetration, called perichoresis, and these relations help to define their personhoods.   Schaab[10] discusses Creation, Incarnation and Grace in an evolving cosmos.   These are all God-World relations.   There is frequent allusion to references of origin, emergence and effect, where creation is one of origin, and an emergent entity by definition cannot be fully described by the forms that constitute it. Several evolutionary species of the cosmos were emergent, and in particular the incarnated Christ and *Homo sapiens*. The Incarnation is a relationship of mutual conditioning between the realities of God and the climax toward which the whole world, or the cosmos, is directed. The anthropic principle, whereby the physical constants of the universe seem finely tuned to the emergence of human intelligent life, constitutes a preparation for the possibility of an Incarnation. In a sense the Trinity and the Incarnation mutually explain each other.   Chapter 8 of Schaab[10] ends by mentioning the Ecumenical Council of Chalcedon definitively asserting in the year 451 AD "the ontological relation between the divine and human natures in the one person of Christ." This confirms our belief!

It is exciting to find so many scholars as well as so many ordinary Christians presently acknowledging their belief in the Triune Godhead!

REPLY BY RON

The concept of the trinity is not easily accepted. How can three persons be one god or one "being"? What does a "person" or "hypostasis" mean? And the Holy Ghost (Spirit)? How does it arise (or "proceed" from the father)? Why should it be necessary to have a father son relationship ("begotten") in a god? The whole thing seems to be an unbelievably complex puzzle. Furthermore, these are not supposed to be merely conceptual "persons" but, in a certain sense, concrete individuals. For example, if Christ was a real person, what was his DNA like? At the time he lived, scientific knowledge of DNA could not even have been thought of. If there was no physical father, where did the DNA come from? This molecule is so complex that it took billions of years to evolve, even for a natural born human. Before we knew about the process of reproduction, this was easier to believe. But now we know the basics by which we are reproduced, the idea of asexual reproduction in humans becomes more and more difficult to accept. Christianity is very old, and as with most old things, its concepts are embedded in the history of our people. Ultimately however, the dead ideas must be discarded and replaced by scientifically acceptable ones. This will not occur suddenly, but over many generations. Nevertheless, it will occur, but the nature of the change has to be in such a way that it is acceptable to people of the faith. It may be that certain concepts now taken as concrete become conceptual. As such, they would not violate scientific discoveries, and yet serve as precepts for behavior. We shall see.

Although many religions have multiple gods, the Trinity represents a unique institution. In the early days of Christianity, little attention was paid to its significance. Hence, early Christianity was much simpler, and easier to understand. People were not bothered by scientific reality. Theophilus of Antioch first mentions the trinity in the late second century, but we would not recognize his definition as our modern day "Trinity". Tertullian early in the third century enunciated father son and Holy Ghost for the first time. Subsequent committees have pondered over what this means and implies. Other religions associate different aspects and abilities to their gods, the Trinity however is the only one to have father son and Holy Ghost, or spirit as such- but what do these really mean? What is written on the significance of these names fills many volumes, but yet, since for most religions these are not concrete objects, it is not at all useful or meaningful and probably a waste of time to devote much effort to discussing whether they have a concrete reality.

Chapter Eleven

Adding a Cubit to Life

INITIAL COMMENTS BY CHARLIE

Verse 6:27 of the Gospel of Matthew presents an interesting enigma!

The original Greek reads: τïς δέ έξ ύμων μεριμνων δυνάται προσθεϊναι επϊ τήν ήλικιάν αυτου πήχυν ένα. The Jerusalem Bible gives a literal translation: "Can any of you, for all his worrying, add one single cubit to his span of life?" as does the New Jerusalem Bible: "Can any of you, however much you worry, add one single cubit to your span of life?" as well as the Revised Standard: "and which of you, by being anxious, can add one cubit to his span of life?" The original Greek, however, is confused because a cubit is a unit of length, the distance from the elbow to the fingertips, which is about a foot and a half or 0.45 meters. It is not a measure of time!

Four of the translations that I checked resolve the confusion by changing lifetime to stature or height:

King James: "Which of you by taking thought, can add one cubit to his stature?"

New English: "Is there a man of you who by anxious thought can add a foot to his height?"

Phillips Modern: "Can any of you, however much he worries, make himself even a few inches taller?"

St. Jerome's late 4th century Latin Vulgate rendition: "Quis autem vestrum cogitans potest adiicere ad staturam suam cubitum unum?" agrees with the KJV above, as does Martin Luther's 1522 German New Testament, "Wer ist aber unter euch, seiner eine Länge eine Elle zusetzen möge, ob er gleich darum sorget?"

In contrast, six other renditions change the word cubit to various lengths of time:

Living Bible: "Will all your worries add a single moment to your life?"

New American: "Can any of you by worrying add a single moment to your life span?"

New International: "Which of you by worrying can add a single hour to your life?"

New Revised Standard: "Can any of you by worrying add a single hour to your span of life?"

Revised English: "Can anxious thought add a single day to your life?"

Today's English: "Which of you can live a few more years by worrying about it?"

The preceding discussion suggests some pertinent observations. For example, what precisely do we mean when we say that Scripture is inerrant? I leave this question to the theologians to ponder. I was surprised at the wide range of deviations from being literal among the various translations. Perhaps in some cases non-literal passages reflect the spirit of the message best. The Latin Vulgate served as the official Catholic version of Scripture for many bygone centuries. The King James Version effectively played this same role for English speaking Protestants during several recent centuries, and is still being widely read by them.

Perhaps the presence of this Cubit anomaly reflects the humanity of the Scripture writers, and that inerrancy lies in the passing on of the true essence of the divine Message from God, and not necessarily its precise original stylistic formulation.

REPLY BY RON

The confusion arising in connection with length and time is of longstanding. I cannot help but think of the woman in the English journal "Punch" stopped by the policeman and accused of speeding because she is going more than 30 miles per hour in a speed zone. She replied, "but officer, that is clearly impossible - I haven't been out an hour!" Furthermore, we now measure astronomical distances in light years. Here we have a combination of time and space. We all know what it means, but it might be confusing to an ignorant casual observer. So far as scripture is concerned, prelates are certainly casual observers when it comes to physics!

Chapter Twelve

The Shroud of Turin

INITIAL COMMENTS BY CHARLIE

The Shroud of Turin is the religious artifact that has been subject to more scientific scrutiny than any other artifact. Many Christians believe that it is the burial cloth of Jesus, and others are convinced that it is a fraud dating from the middle ages. The burial cloth claim became dubious after the announcement in 1988 of the results of the Carbon-14 dating:

Age = 1325 AD, between 1292 and 1358 with a 66% probability

The three laboratories in Arizona, Oxford and Zürich that did the dating were all in agreement with the reported results. The Shroud had appeared in Lirey, France, in 1357, at the upper limit of the 66% probability range. I call the claims dubious because some supporters of a 2000 year age claim that the dating was erroneous due an improper choice of sample location, residues from the 1532 fire, microbial contamination, or a natural fungus-like organic coating on the fibers. There were also pollen grains from the Middle East found on it. In my opinion the prudent thing to do is to accept the Shroud as a linen cloth from the Middle East dating from the14[th] century, which has a controversial image, imprinted on it.

Even if we agree to judge the Shroud as only about 700 years old it is still not reasonable to label it as a fraud. It simply has too many mysteries and unexplained features associated with it. There is no sign of paint or of any other artificial staining material on the cloth. Its image arose from a chemical change in the cellulose structure on the surface of the linen fibers. This resulted from a dehydrative-oxidative process that could never have been brought about by a mediaeval artist. There are, however, blood stains at expected locations. There are in addition some fascinating details. All the body dimensions are anatomically correct. The nail wound is through the wrist whereas almost all the artwork has this wound through the palm of the hand where the nail could never support the weight of a crucified man. When the nail is hammered into a person's wrist it causes the thumb to fold into the palm which explains why the Shroud exhibits hands with only four fingers showing. The arms show blood flowing in two directions corresponding to the crucified man successively raising his body to breathe and lowering it to rest. It is extremely unlikely that a mediaeval artist would know these details. In addition the image is a negative, and negative images were unknown until the advent of photography in the 19th century. It also exhibits three-dimensional features never found in an artificial image such as a painting. All of this makes it almost impossible to imagine how someone could have fabricated this image during the fourteenth century.

In my capacity as a deacon hoping to find some authenticity of the Crucifixion of Jesus in the Shroud, and as a physicist trusting the results of the various scientific studies including the carbon-14 dating, I ponder what it all means. It is the mentality of scientists to propose theories that provide reasonable explanations of all the phenomena observed in nature. In the case of the Shroud, despite the extensive scientific investigations and measurements that have been carried out no reasonable scientific explanation has emerged. The image is simply an unexplained mystery, or more precisely a mystery lacking any reasonable scientific explanation. It seems to me, in my capacity of being a scientist who is a believing Christian, that the most likely and the most believable explanation is that the image was miraculously imprinted on a herringbone weave linen cloth dating from the Middle East sometime between the year 1325 AD and the year 1357 AD. This means that at the beginning of this article I erred by referring to the Shroud as an artifact. I apologize for this.

At the present time there are sharp divergences of opinion concerning the authenticity and the significance of the Shroud of Turin. One extreme accepts it as the actual burial cloth of Jesus, while the opposite extreme dismisses it a fraud. Neither extreme has proponents who are urging a repeat of the carbon-14 dating on a mutually agreed upon sample from the original shroud, perhaps purged of possible contaminants, or on other ancient linen cloths deliberately so-contaminated. Neither side seems anxious for more validation! We believe that our more moderate explanation best conforms to the known facts about the Shroud with no need of a repeat of the dating.

RESPONSE BY RON

The shroud of Turin represents an interesting puzzle but little more. Were we to take such relics seriously, there are many more similar strange objects which are venerated as religious. As an example, take the bones of St. Peter, which only recently have been put on display in the Vatican. Carbon dating has proved them to be of the right era, but nevertheless, one must be extremely cautious about true authentication. Still, millions of pilgrims come annually to venerate the relics now on view, so it behooves those in charge of them to treat the pilgrims with respect.

Chapter Thirteen

The Inquisition, Crusades, and Imprecatoria

INITIAL COMMENTS BY CHARLIE.

In recent years Western nations have felt threatened by acts of violence committed by Islamic extremists. Examples of this are recurring suicide bomber incidents, and the earlier 9/11 attacks on the New York World Trade Center buildings. It is suggested that the mentality that motivates the perpetrators of these crimes is similar to that which existed in Christianity during the times of the Inquisition and the Crusades. It is further noted that Christianity has largely outgrown this mentality, and it is time for Islam to do the same. After all, every sura or chapter in the Qur'an, except #9 entitled Repentance, begins with the invocation "In the Name of Allah, the Beneficent, the Merciful!"

PROSELYTISM

The word "proselytize" means to attempt to convert someone from one cause to another, or more specifically from one religion to another. Islam and Christianity are the two main proselytizing religions of the world. They both divide the world into believers and non-believers, and they both have the ambition to proselytize and to convert all non-believers. The Gospel of Matthew (28:18) ends with the commission:

Go ye, therefore, and teach all nations, baptizing them in the name of the Father, and of the Son, and of the Holy Spirit

(KJV)

and we read in Sura 47:11 of the Qur'an:

This is because Allah is a patron of those who believe, And because disbelievers have no patron.

Both religions believe that conversion is irrevocable. For example, baptism puts an indelible mark on the soul that can never be removed. A child should not be baptized unless there is a reasonable expectation that he or she will be brought up as a Christian. If a person renounces Islam in a Sharia law country, he or she can be legally put to death. In a non-Sharia law country many members of a Muslim community residing there would not object to the killing of a Muslim apostate. It is also true that both religions object to forced conversions. Thus Sura 2:256 of the Qur'an says explicitly "there is no compulsion in religion" so a Muslim apostate who can prove that his conversion was forced on him is automatically released from the death penalty. Unfortunately, the commission of Sura 2:256 applies only to non-Muslims; there is a very strong intimidation on Muslims to remain so!

Muslims believe that People of the Book, namely Jews, Christians and Zoroastrians, all had received valid prior revelations or scriptures from Allah/God, but these have been corrupted and superseded by the Qur'an, the final 'true' divine Revelation made to the 'final Prophet' Muhammad. It seems strange that the Qur'an never once makes mention of Elijah, Ezekiel, Isaiah, or Jeremiah, the main prophets of the Old Testament. They simply do not exist in Islamic scripture or tradition.

NO SALVATION OUTSIDE THE CHURCH

In the third century St. Cyprian of Carthage asserted *Extra Ecclesiam nulla salus* meaning "Outside the Church there is no salvation," and this axiom has been repeated by many

Church leaders down through the centuries. This proposition was proclaimed officially at the Fourth Lateran Council in the year 1215. More recently at the Second Vatican Council (1965) it was reformulated positively, it means that all salvation comes from Christ the Head through the Church, which is his body

The axiom has received various interpretations throughout history, and literal interpretations have strongly motivated vigorous missionary endeavors to convert the entire world. They also motivated taking strong measures to ensure that no one renounces the faith or preaches doctrines contrary to the official teachings of the Church.

THE INQUISITION

A result of a very literal interpretation of the *Extra Ecclesiam* axiom was the establishment by Catholicism in the 12th century of an official institution called the Inquisition. The emblem of the Inquisition was a quotation from Psalm 94: *Exurge Domine et Judica Causam Tuam* meaning "Arise Lord and Judge Your Cause." The Inquisition was commissioned to maintain and defend the integrity of the faith by investigating and proscribing false doctrines and errors. More specifically it sought to induce all heretics to recant, and to punish those who refused to do so. Galileo was one of the famous victims of the Inquisition. The Inquisition only had jurisdiction over baptized members of the Church, but non-Christians could be tried for blasphemy by civil courts. Blasphemy is also a very serious crime in Sharia-law countries, and has been used as an excuse to harass disbelievers. Since the Church as an institution does not inflict corporal punishment on anyone the ancient custom was to turn the guilty person over to the civil authorities who carried out the punishment. For an unrepentant heretic the punishment was sometimes burning at the stake. These punishments were carried out publicly with the intention of deterring others from falling into heresy in the future.

Unfortunately, torture was at times utilized, but with three restrictions: (a) it could only be applied one time, (b) it could be used to help induce a heretic to confess, but never as a punishment after pronouncing a guilty verdict, and (c) it was not allowed to cause any permanent harm to the person. That is why the rack was often chosen as the instrument of torture; it inflicts great pain that can be gradually intensified, but when properly administered it produces no permanent physical harm. Unfortunately, it was not always properly administered.

An inquisitorial trial often ended with a public celebration called an *auto de fé, which* involved a High Mass, some prayers, and a procession of those found guilty followed by a reading of their sentences. High-level ecclesiastical and civil authorities were often in attendance.

Official policies to suppress heresy were also implemented in some Protestant states such as by the theocracy established by John Calvin in Geneva during the 16th century. In recent centuries all of Christianity has given up the utilization of coercion to suppress heresy and to punish heretics. Islam has always had and still has a determination to maintain and defend the integrity of its faith by investigating and proscribing false doctrines and errors, using intimidation and force when necessary. It is time for Islam to emulate Christianity by forsaking the use of coercion and death threats to prevent individuals from discontinuing to believe in Islam.

If a Muslim in a Sharia Law country decides to renounce his belief in Islam he will be asked to reconsider, and will be granted some time to do so. He will be examined by a psychiatrist to make sure that he is sane, and if he persists in his unbelief his Muslim wife can be forced to divorce him, his children can be taken away, and his property can be confiscated. Worst of all he can be brought to court and sentenced to death for apostasy. If he repents later he is spared from death and can return to his old life. Thus the status of an apostate in Islam is quite similar to that of an unrepentant heretic convicted by an inquisitorial court several centuries ago. Christianity has succeeded in attaining a high enough level of civilization to eradicate the death penalty for heresy, but Islam has not yet reached this level of civilized development. It is time for it to do so, and to agree that the decree of Sura 2:256, mentioned above, applies to Muslims as well as to non-Muslims.

THE CRUSADES

The Eastern Crusades were military expeditions undertaken from the 11th to the 13th centuries by Christian volunteers to retake the Holy Places in the Middle East that had been seized from Christianity by Muslims several hundred years earlier. Their object was to make Sacred Places such as the Holy Sepulcher safe havens for Christian pilgrims to visit. The Crusades were announced by preaching, and various kings, princes and individual warriors took solemn vows to embark on them. Crusaders received special indulgences and some temporal privileges for their participation. The initial Crusades were undertaken because Christians found that a pilgrimage to the Holy Land had become a very unsafe and hazardous undertaking, and some pilgrims never returned home alive. During the 12th and 13th centuries much of the land of Palestine was in the hands of Christians, with many interchanges of individual sovereignties between Christian and Muslim territories taking place during that period. The Christian presence in the Holy Land came to an end in the year 1291 when the Christian Kingdom of Jerusalem ceased to exist.

The attitude of Islam relative to the state of Israel is quite similar to what had been the attitude of the Crusaders relative to the land of Palestine some eight hundred years ago. Islam wants to get back the territory that was taken from it by the Jewish people when they established the state of Israel in 1948. In particular, they want full sovereignty over the holy city of Jerusalem where they claim Muhammad made his ascent into heaven. Many would probably be willing to inflict as much violence and loss of life as may be necessary to regain possession of Palestine and the holy city of Jerusalem. In this sense they would be imitating the Crusaders who did not shy away from inflicting violence when it was deemed necessary. From a broader perspective the three Abrahamic religions have been spending much of the previous 1,400 years fighting over territory that is sacred to all three of them. At the present time many Christians support Israel because they believe that their Christian shrines such as the Holy Sepulcher are more readily accessible to them under Jewish control than they would be under Muslim control.

Perhaps the most significant development and change in attitude of Christians during the past few hundred years has been their renunciation of the posture of violence to regain what Islam had seized from them many centuries earlier, such as several cities to which St. Paul wrote letters, and cities such as Nicaea where Ecumenical Councils were held. For example, in the year 1453 Muslim armies captured the city of Constantinople and converted the great church Hagia Sophia into a mosque, which it remained for 481 years. Prior to its seizure by Islam by force of arms Hagia Sophia had been the second most important church in Christendom for almost a millennium. The impact of this desecration on Christianity is equivalent to what would be the impact on Islam if a Christian army conquered Mecca and converted the Ka'aba into a Christian church, and keeping it that way for 481 years. In my opinion the Republic of Turkey should return Hagia Sophia to the Orthodox Church, and Islam as an Abrahamic religion should renounce the use of violence, and accept the presence of the sovereign state of Israel in the land of Palestine. Christianity went through its period of terror and violence to regain Muslim territory, and Islam must now bring its posture of terror and violence to an end!

IMPRECATORY PRAYER

Imprecatory psalms such as the 35th and 109th pronounce a curse over enemies of the Lord or of the Lord's people, as in the following selection from verses 12 to 15 of the latter psalm:

> Let no one treat him kindly, or pity his fatherless children May his posterity be destroyed, his name cease in the next generation May the Lord remember his father's guilt, his mother's sin not be cancelled. May their guilt be always before the Lord till their memory is banished from the earth.

There are other imprecatory passages in the Old Testament, such as in the book of Joshua. The Qur'an also has many imprecatory suras or chapters, as in verse 68 of sura 9:

> Allah promiseth the hypocrites, both men and women, and the disbelievers in their abode. It will suffice them. Allah curseth them, and theirs is lasting torment

In verse 6 of sura 98 we read:

> Lo those who disbelieve, among the People of the Scripture and the idolaters, will abide in fire of hell.

> They are the worst of created beings.

At the Second Vatican Council a decision was made to omit imprecatory passages from the official prayers of the Church in the Divine Office because they are not conducive to the fostering of a devout prayer life. When Muslims pray the Qur'an in their daily prayers they make no attempt to systematically omit imprecatory passages. They include in their prayers not only harsh verses about the treatment of disbelievers, but also warlike or jihad type verses such as sura 2:191:

> And slay them wherever you find them and drive them out of the places where they drove you out, for persecution is worse than slaughter. And fight not with them at the inviolable Place of Worship until they attack you there, but if they attack you there then slay them. Such is the reward of disbelievers.

In response to this one might inquire: How would Muslims react if Christians included in their prayers verses such as "Muslims are the worst of created beings. God curses them, and theirs is a lasting torment?" One also wonders what effect the inclusion of these imprecatory suras in the daily prayers of Muslims has on their attitude toward Christians, and what effect it has on their support for suicide bombings. Prayer should be a time for seeking forgiveness for our sins, not a time for cursing our neighbor. It is time for Islam to follow the lead of Christianity by eliminating imprecatory material from their prayer life.

CONCLUDING REMARK

Christians, Jews and Zoroastrians alike look forward to a possible future era when the People of the Qur'an will honor Allah by displaying His Beneficence and His Mercy in their dealings with the People of the Book. From the viewpoint of Islam may Allah and His messenger Muhammad be praised, and from the viewpoint of Christianity let the Father, the Son, and the Holy Spirit be praised. Amen!

REPLY BY RON

It would seem that the attitude of many, if not most religions, is that the only way to ensure the prevalence of their beliefs is to kill everyone else. This in spite of the edicts of the founder of that religion. It is only recently that members of any sect realize it is better to live and let live. Nine eleven has shown this has not penetrated to many Muslims. Time will tell however, and a better education will help.

PROSELYTISM

Religions propagate by proselytizing. Few do not proselytize, Judaism and Unitarian-Universalists (UUS) being two such, which is probably why the UUs are so few. Aggressive proselytization can lead to problems however. When I was in Australia, I had close friends who were anthropologists, and used to go up to the South Sea Islands on research. They had horror stories about the problems the missionaries, particularly the nonconformists such as the Baptists caused. Specifically, the tradition amongst the islanders was if the husband of one of the inhabitants died, his widow would become a second wife to the husband of her sister. This arrangement appeared to work very well. The missionaries however, demanded that Christianity permitted only one wife. The net result was the unfortunate widow found she had no place in society, and committed suicide. There were a number of similar instances. Nevertheless, no doubt Christianity brought the islanders into the modern world.

NO SALVATION OUTSIDE THE CHURCH

Firstly, one has to believe in salvation. Christianity makes a big point of salvation. The UUs do not. I believe it was Mark Twain who said that sitting on a cloud playing a harp did not appeal to him. He also said he felt half his friends were in hell, and half in heaven. He would go to heaven for the environment, but hell for the company.

THE INQUISITION

To most modern Americans, the Inquisition brings to mind the Monty Python show, where these red clothed individuals enter and say, "We are the Spanish Inquisition. Prepare to be tortured". From being one of the most feared products of the Catholic Church, to being a joke on television is quite a jump. Nevertheless, the early church wanted to keep its beliefs pure, so it set up a system to punish what it considered perverters of the faith. Since the accused were not allowed to know their accusers before the trial, it must inevitably have led to corruption from people wanting to get rid of an unwanted neighbor, or merely someone they did not like. At least ten thousand victims were executed, many by burning, over the years. The Inquisition was not finally done away with until the nineteenth century, and vestiges of it still remain in the form of being thrown out of the church for various reasons. Other religions, such as the Muslims, still maintain a "jihad", or "holy war" against all other religions. This can be either military or non-military. The military jihad differs little from the crusades, and, in the form of the Muslim brotherhood, is basically a terrorist organization. This has caused an immense amount of suffering in those countries where the Muslim religion is dominant. As mentioned earlier, the Muslims are socially about where the Christian religion was at the time of the crusades.

THE CRUSADES

The Crusades are one of the anachronisms of Christianity. In the tenth through thirteenth centuries, there was a publicity campaign "get back Jerusalem and the Holy Land". Like many publicity campaigns it was largely false, but it encouraged wealthy people - even the king of England to embark on hazardous and costly expeditions. Some were clearly very peculiar. Take the "children's crusade" as an example. Firstly it is not entirely clear whether this really occurred, but if it did, the children never got to the holy land, and it is likely they would have been killed if they had. Instead, it seems most likely they were sold into slavery in North Africa. Come what may, it was a bad idea from the start. The "Knights Templar" was another wealthy organization connected with the Crusades, and it too ultimately vanished-except for books and movies - also generally incorporating a search for the "Holy Grail" out of which Christ drank at the last supper.

IMPRECATORY PRAYERS

Imprecatory prayers require that you believe that there is a god who is able to reward you for killing god's enemies. The prayers are merely the incentive to proceed with the process. Similarly, if you pray to God for money, and he responds, then you have a personal god whom it would obviously be advantageous to placate. Many people believe in such a god, and clearly this is one reason we have so many religious wars. In many cases, it is in the financial interest of the people promoting the war that it should be carried on, irrespective of the number of people killed. The prophet of the religion would most likely be against such warfare, but, being dead, can't complain. As Poole mentions, imprecatory prayers are gradually dying out, and hopefully, as time goes on will be replaced by more productive invocations.

Chapter Fourteen

Abortion and Euthanasia

INITIAL COMMENTS BY CHARLIE

In this essay we will talk about both early abortions that take place before, as well as late abortions that take place after, the eighth week of gestation when the embryo begins to be called a fetus, which is another name for an as-yet unborn baby. We approach the situation from a scientific perspective. After fertilization the ovum of the mother is called a zygote. It consists of one cell, which splits into two cells, then four ells, eight cells, etc. After four subdivisions the cells cluster forming a structure called a blastocyst. This structure travels to the uterus where it forms a placenta and implants in the uterine wall beginning about the fifth day after fertilization. The embryo then develops into the fetus. By the end of the eighth week the brain is completely present and "the beginnings of all the main organ systems have been established." (K. L. Moore and T. V. N. Persaud, The Developing Human, Clinically Oriented Embryology, p. 91). Prior to this, heartbeats are detectible at three weeks, brain waves at six weeks, and the mother can feel movements of the baby, a phenomenon called quickening, at six weeks. Since all main organ systems have been established at eight weeks and what remains is growth, the unborn has now reached the status of incipient babyhood. At this stage the fetus has begun to look like a baby, with a head, face, arms and legs, etc. Thus after eight weeks of formation he or she can legitimately be called a baby. Between 24 and 28 weeks the baby becomes viable, that is, it has a reasonable probability to live outside the womb.

Scientifically it is evident that all babies are the same human beings whether they are prematurely born, newly born, six months old or two years old. They are also, scientifically speaking, the same babies whether they are still in the womb, or have undergone a birth. This is a scientific fact that must be acknowledged by all who respect the authority of science. It is a crime called first-degree murder to kill an already born baby for the convenience of the mother, and likewise it should be a crime of first-degree murder to kill a baby in the womb simply for the convenience of the mother. It is incredible that in our so-called civilized society babies before they are born are considered as somehow inferior to their already born brothers and sisters, and hence subject to being killed arbitrarily.

This is extremely unjust, and is reminiscent of what used to be the status of slaves. It was also the status of Jews and Gypsies in Nazi Germany, and is presently the status of Muslims who convert to Christianity in Islamic countries. All of these cases are contrary to what science teaches us about the intrinsic dignity of all human beings, and hence their right to life.

The partial birth abortion controversy as well as the Holocaust illustrated the incredible cruelty that can be practiced by civilized human beings when dealing with a class of humans judged to be inferior and hence subject to arbitrary killing. When implementing this partial birth abortion procedure, the entire body of the full-grown baby was allowed to exit from the womb so that only the head remained inside. An incision was then made at the base of the skull and the brain was suctioned out, thereby killing the baby in a very cruel and painful manner. The head of the deceased baby then exited the womb, bringing to a close the partial birth infanticide. This was clearly an act of barbarism. Fortunately the procedure was outlawed by the Partial-Birth Abortion Act of 2003.

I find it incredible that our legal system has been unwilling to accept second and third trimester fetuses as real 100% babies to be legally treated as such. I also find it incredible that no scientists or medical professionals have spoken out publically in protest to this absurdity!

Thus it is now clear why late term abortions should never be allowed, so we will pass on to consider the case of the early term variety, i.e. those which occur prior to the end of the eighth week of gestation. At conception the fertilized ovum or zygote acquires the characteristic DNA of a human being. This means that the embryo is 100% human, which should be enough to make it immune from being killed. When an animal such as a butterfly is on the endangered species list it is not only a crime to kill it, but it is also a crime to kill its eggs, its corresponding cater- pillar, and its pupa in the cocoon. It is clear that a baby after birth is much more precious than a butterfly, and hence it should be acknowledged that a human fetus or embryo is much more precious than a caterpillar. What applies to the early life stages of a butterfly should, *a fortiori*, apply to the early life stages in the life of a human being. Hence it is important to reiterate and emphasize that we human beings are intrinsically more precious than butterflies, and hence our human embryos are intrinsically more precious than caterpillars and pupae. Is the present situation an example of hypocrisy or not? In my status as a physicist I feel strongly that we should pay attention to the logical conclusions of our science!

REPLY BY RON

The concept of abortion raises the ire of many of us. Conservatives accuse us of taking human life, liberals of paying no attention to the wishes desires or medical requirements of the pregnant female. Whichever side you take you are bound to find strong proponents and opponents. Partly this is because, where human life is concerned, we all have strong feelings. Under British law, the critical quantity was "quickening". This was when the woman first felt the fetus move, and realized for sure she was pregnant. Up to that time steps could be taken to abort. The medical procedure of "D and C" (dilation and curettage) can also be used under the subterfuge that this is necessary for other reasons.

The trouble with abortion is that everyone is against it, except for those whose lives will be ruined unless they procure one immediately.

We must examine the psychological requirements for abortion, as well as the medical ones. If a woman gets pregnant accidentally, are we to ruin her whole life by demanding she must carry an unwanted pregnancy to term? If the baby is unwanted, it does not set a good precedent for its future life, although of course there is the possibility of a good adoption

The problem of partial birth abortion places the physician on the horns of a dilemma. Essentialy this arises when the fetus cannot get born without killing the mother, leading to the problem of which is to die. The grisly procedure in which the fetus is dragged through the birth canal, cutting the head open to allow its passage is fairly rare, but still amounts to a few thousand a year. The attitude of the Catholic Church is that we should leave it to fate, and not help to influence the result. It is so difficult to determine whether such abortion is necessary that perhaps the decision should be left to the woman, since should she not die, presumably she could bear more children.

It is interesting to note perhaps that while the Catholic Church is strongly opposed to any form of abortion, its view on the artificial prolongation of life are somewhat different - they believe one should not prolong life artificially.

Chapter Fifteen

Reacting to Same-Sex Marriage

COMMENTS BY CHARLIE

In recent years the lesbian, gay, bisexual, transgender, or LGBT homosexual community has been engaged in a campaign to have their gay marriages accepted as equal in validity to the usual heterosexual ones. Gallup poll results indicated that the percentage of public support for this has been continually rising, and has exceeded 50% since the year 2011. The question that now confronts me is how I, as a mature heterosexual man who opposes same-sex marriage, should react to this situation. Before addressing this question, a very unusual personal experience will be recounted.

OUR WHOLE BEING RESPONDS TO SEX

In about the year 1980, when I was 52 years old, I was running a 10 K race, and after several minutes all the runners had become quite spread out, with each running at a comfortable pace. When I looked ahead of me I caught sight of a competitor in the distance running at the same pace as myself, and I was unable to distinguish whether or not the runner was male or female. This made me feel very uneasy. My usual 10K racing time was 47 minutes, so I spent the next 40 or 42 minutes staring at this person feeling more and more awkward every minute, and not understanding why. The runner was too far ahead for me to think about wasting energy to catch up. Thus there wasn't much else to do except to look at him/her as I ran along, and the unpleasant awkward feeling made me keep focusing my attention trying to detect some indication of the runner's gender. She turned out to be a woman in her late thirties so she was not competing with me for an age-group award. The whole experience made me realize that we really are sexual creatures and this influences the way we react to each other. We are all sexual creatures living in a world populated by roughly equal numbers of men and women.

HOW MANY GENDERS ARE THERE?

We inhabit a world that is traditionally considered as populated by two groups of people, namely males (M) and females (F), which constitute the two sexes or genders. Men and women differ from each other biologically, psychologically, and sociologically, and they also differ from each other in the variety of their sexual attractions. Most men are attracted toward women and most women are attracted toward men, so they are referred to as heterosexual individuals. As a result it is common for a man and a woman to unite in an association called a marriage so they can live together, engage in sexual activity, and beget children. This is why until the present era everyone has agreed to define marriage in terms of the two genders that comprise it, namely one man and one woman.

In addition to the dominant heterosexual community there is a minority of the population in the LGBT community. According to the Williams Institute Review this community constitutes only 3.8% of the overall population of the United States (1.7% gay & lesbian, 1.8% bisexual, and 0.3 % transgender). These men, referred to as gay (G), are sexually attracted to other men, and these women, referred to as lesbians (L), are sexually attracted to other women. It is in our era common for a pair of homosexuals to form an association, live together, engage in sexual activity, and perhaps adopt children. They are presently campaigning to have their unions accepted as valid marriages, either a gay marriage uniting two gay men, or a lesbian marriage uniting two lesbian women. In other words since a marriage is defined by the genders of the individual that constitute it, by seeking marriage unions these homosexuals are acting like they constitute separate genders, namely gay and lesbian. There are also bisexual people who experience a sexual attraction to both men and women, and a fourth group called transgender individuals whose defining characteristics are not totally clear to me. In other words this lesbian, gay, bisexual, transgender or LGBT community appears anxious to characterize the world as populated by people with six different orientations with respect to gender, and this seems equivalent to postulating that there are six different genders, namely M, F, L, G, B and T. These genders are ordinarily permanent throughout a person's lifetime, although there have been cases in which a change has occurred from, for example, bisexual to transgender. In such a world everyone would be classified by gender, and there would be some changes in perspectives. For example, a particular homosexual man's driver's license might be stamped: "Sex: G" instead of "Sex: M."

In our present two-gender world there are some cases in which gender differences are taken into account, and other cases in which they are not considered. In my sport of running separate awards are given to men and women to take into account the intrinsic difference in the strengths of their bodies. In my profession of academia men and women compete directly against each other because there is no intrinsic difference in their levels of intelligence. In this article we shall argue against the recognition of an effective six-dimensional world of gender. We believe that it is important for the various members of the LGBT community to become acclimated to and welcomed by our two-gender world, and the recognition of homosexual marriages as valid marriages would be a step in the wrong direction.

THE CONSEQUENCES OF A SIX-GENDER WORLDVIEW

In a six-gender world children in their formative years, namely those in grammar-school, middle-school, and high-school, will find themselves experimenting with different types of sexual activities as they seek to establish their sexual identities from among six available choices: The idea that these students, our children and our grandchildren (I have 15), would engage in various varieties of sexual behavior to help them to determine and establish their sexual identity from among these six options is repugnant to most people. The majority of the population simply does not want their children and grandchildren being brought up in this kind of sexually permissive environment. Most of them much prefer to have virginity and the abstinence from sexual behavior until marriage as the norm that is universally agreed upon, and fostered in our school system. We believe that a return to this former cultural environment is desirable. When the members of the present older generation were young they lived in a world in which it was considered proper for everyone, but especially for women, to remain virgins until they entered into marriage with a person of the opposite gender. We now live in a much more permissive or unrestricted cultural environment in which many people feel that it is perfectly all right to live together before marriage. We advocate pursuing policies that will foster a return to the prior much less permissive code of sexual morality, and we believe that the acceptance of homosexual marriages could hinder us from achieving this goal.

END ALL PREJUDICE AGAINST GAYS AND LESBIANS

Concerning our brothers and sisters who are lesbian, gay, bisexual, or transgender we endorse the statement in the Catechism of the Catholic Church (#23580): "They must be accepted with respect, compassion, and sensitivity. Every sign of unjust discrimination in their regard should be avoided." Thus individuals who are homosexual must be treated with the same respect as individuals who are heterosexual. The same, of course, applies to those who are bisexual or transgender.

HANDICAPS, DISABILITIES, AND DISORDERS

There are many people who have what can be called handicaps, disabilities or impairments (disorders). Examples are the blind, the mute (deaf), and the lame. In recent years many cities have modified their sidewalks to make them wheelchair negotiable, and ramps have been added to buildings to make them wheelchair accessible. The general public has been very supportive of this. In past years homosexuality had been effectively a handicap because the prejudice against this group was so widespread that in many cases their adherents had difficulty obtaining and maintaining gainful employment. Fortunately, this is no longer universally the case. It is much to the credit of the LGBT community that they have succeeded in overcoming much of this prejudice, and in establishing themselves as worthwhile contributors to modern American culture. We heterosexuals should rejoice at this, and we should congratulate our LGBT associates for this accomplishment.

HOMOSEXALITY AND NORMALITY

Several years ago I, a heterosexual, became interested in learning more about the Gay/Lesbian community because of my interest in the Gay marriage controversy. Accordingly, I read two very informative books: 1) *The Gay Militants* (1971) by Donn Teal and, 2) *Making History; The Struggle for Gay & Lesbian Equal Rights* (1992) by Eric Marcus, and I found out that members of the LGBT community experienced the same type of rejection by so called "ordinary people" that I had experienced in my youth when I was a pronounced stutterer. I found out that members of both communities are anxious to learn the identities of fellow members who had become famous for accomplishing great things in their lifetimes, despite their handicaps. In addition they both loathed the rejection that they received from so-called ordinary people. One major difference between these communities is the fact that stutterers, as well as blind, mute, and lame people, rejoice when one of their members achieves what might be called a "cure" and becomes normal with no remaining disability, and others of their kind are encouraged to also seek such cures. In contrast to this in the gay/lesbian community there is a strong opposition to one of its members undergoing any type of treatment to become "straight." I am unable to comprehend the rationale for this attitude. It probably results from the desire of the members of the LGBT community to have homosexuality and heterosexuality classified together with bisexuality and transgender as alternate varieties of normality. I doubt very much that the heterosexual community will ever be receptive to this type of designation!

Prior to the year 1973 The American Psychiatric Association (APA) had listed homosexuality as a "sociopathic personality disorder" in their Diagnostics & Statistical Manual (DSM), and the LGBT community successfully campaigned to induce them to remove this designation from the Manual by disrupting various public meetings of the APA. This demonstrates how determined they are to eventually convince the general public to regard homosexuality and heterosexuality as two equally normal varieties of sexuality. I, myself, was glad when I found out that stuttering was a symptom of a neurosis, as this helped me to overcome the disorder.

WHAT SCRIPTURE AND TRADITION PROCLAIM

It is important to point out that the New Testament, in the words of St. Paul, explicitly designates adultery, fornication, and sodomy as grievous offenses against the law of God. Christian preachers have a right and a duty to proclaim this teaching by the freedom of religion statutes of the U. S. Constitution's Bill of Rights, and no one has the right to deny them this privilege.

In the sixteenth century the Protestant Reformers based their Reformation on the principle of *Sola Scriptura*, the literal acceptance of what Scripture tell us. Catholics in their subsequent Counter-Reformation insisted that the Church continue to proclaim the Gospel as it was proclaimed by the Apostolic Church of the early centuries. This Protestant emphasis on the primacy of Scripture and the Catholic joint emphasis on the primacies of Scripture as well as Tradition led each of them to endorse the same strict code of sexual morality. They both accepted the truth of the proclamation of St. Paul that "adultery, fornication, and sodomy are grievous offenses against the law of God." Thus, according to the Scriptures, it is wrong for an unmarried heterosexual couple to live together and engage in acts of sexual intimacy, and it is equally wrong for a homosexual couple to live together and engage in acts of sexual intimacy.

From another perspective, our generation seems to be the first in history in which many people have not only rejected the judgment of St. Paul concerning the sinful trilogy "adultery, fornication, and sodomy," but many have even raised some of these actions to the status of virtues to be desired and praised. Events such as "celebrations of diversity" tend to do this. Sodomy acquires this status in a homosexual marriage, and fornication acquires this status when a heterosexual couple lives together in a trial marriage designed to assess compatibility. In addition, adultery sometimes acquires this status when a husband, experiencing problems with his wife, seeks consolation from another woman. Modern secular society often accepts the first two as laudatory, and occasionally accepts the third as such, depending upon the circumstances. Thus Christianity confronts a new paganism in the form of secularism, which seeks to hinder its ability to proclaim the Gospel against the present atmosphere of sexual permissiveness.

It is the duty of priests, ministers and other officials in leadership positions of Christian churches to proclaim these doctrines, and to urge their faithful to abide by them in their personal lives. Unfortunately at the present time there are some Christian denominations which are permitting ministers and bishops to live together with homosexual partners, which recalls the words of St. Paul in 2 Tim 4:3 "For the time will come when people will not tolerate sound doctrine but, following their own desires, and insatiable curiosity, they will stop listening to the truth and will be diverted by myths." It is fortunate that most of Christianity is remaining faithful to the teachings of Scripture, and disheartening that several influential branches or denominations are being "diverted by myths." If St. Paul were alive today he would be writing epistles to these latter denominations urging their return to orthodoxy and sound doctrine.

INCLINATION VERSUS ACTS

In treating the subject of homosexuality it is necessary to distinguish between homosexual inclinations or tendencies, and homosexual actions or acts. The inclination involves a sexual attraction toward persons of the same sex that can be predominant, or in some cases exclusive. It can constitute a trial to the 3.8 percent of the population that experience it. However in no way can any blame be ascribed to individuals with this inclination. Bisexual individuals experience sexual attraction toward both males and females. In like manner there can also be no blame for having this type of inclination, and both types of individuals should be able to live their lives free from any variety of discrimination for their inclinations. This was not the case during and prior to the 21st century when many neighbors and prospective employers openly and/or covertly discriminated against homosexual, bisexual, and transgender individuals. Fortunately in the present 22nd century this has largely, but not yet completely, come to an end.

As far as homosexual acts are concerned they were considered reprehensible by most people in earlier generations, and as was mentioned above, St. Paul admonishes against committing acts of adultery, fornication and sodomy with equal vigor, and with a strong emphasis.

Many in the LGBT community find this very disturbing, and some of them have acquired animosities against the branches of Christianity that take these admonitions of St. Paul very seriously. We call upon members of the LGBT community to denounce the demonization of Christians who publicly support all the teachings of S. Paul.

BREAKDOWN OF MORALITY

At the present time many heterosexual couples are cohabiting, or living together without being married, as well as in many cases giving birth to children. For example, in the year 2012 the astonishing total of 40.7% of all the births in the United States was out of wedlock. In recent years (see Ventura and Bachrach, National Vital Statistics Reports 18) this statistic has undergone a gradual annual increase from 6% in 1960, to 10% in 1970, 16% in 1980, 27% in 1990, 35% in 2000, and finally to the value mentioned above of 40.7% in the year 2012. In this particular year the figure for out-of wedlock births was 72% for blacks, 54% for Hispanics, 29% for Caucasians, and only 17% for Asians-Pacific Islanders. Christians and many others find this overall situation very disturbing, and the leaders of the various Christians denominations are very anxious to counteract and reverse this relatively recent progressive breakdown in sexual morality. It is important for all of us to recognize the critical role of the traditional marriage family as the fundamental building block of a sustainable society, and need to direct sexual activity and mores accordingly.

RETURN TO THE EARLY CHURCH

It thus appears that the sexual morality of secular society is at present rapidly reverting to the low level that had prevailed during the first few centuries AD when Christianity was undergoing its early establishment and growth in the Roman Empire. It is now appropriate for the various denominations to resolve their differences and return to a greater unity and fellowship. Christianity once again has the task of preaching worldwide the Gospel of Jesus Christ our Savior and Redeemer, and of once again bringing back humanity toward adherence to the more chaste code of sexual morality that had prevailed when our parents and grand parents were growing up! This is indeed a real challenge for us.

PROPOSED RETURN TO A STRICT CODE OF SEXUAL MORALITY

Christians, of course, do not have a right to impose their code of morality on society. They can, however, legitimately urge a return of society to a much stricter code of sexual ethics by basing their arguments on reason rather than on scripture, and this is our intention. It was mentioned above that a large percentage of the older generation is very disturbed by the prospect of their children and grandchildren being brought up in a prevailing atmosphere of unrestricted sexual freedom. We need a return to a cultural environment in which almost every live birth is to a married woman, and single moms become a rarity. We must return to a society that dignifies long-lasting marriages endowed with multiple children to offset the present-day unhealthy population decreases that are presently taking place in many countries around the world. The injection of the phenomenon of gay marriages into our culture when what is most needed is an emphasis on reinforcing healthy heterosexual marriages will serve to divert us from bringing about the return to a strict conventional code of morality in society.

THE OPPRESSED BECOMES THE OPPRESSOR

It is a common phenomenon that when a formerly oppressed group achieves power then its members sometimes become the oppressors of their former opponents. This happened at the end of the eighteenth century when the French revolution led to a bloodbath. It happened in the United States after the 1972 Roe v. Wade Supreme Court decision that legalized unrestricted abortions. At that time many pro-choice leaders were anxious to force all hospitals to perform abortions, and to make it mandatory for all physicians and nurses to be willing to participate in the performance of abortions even when they believed an abortion to be an act of murder. More recently in England pro-life adoption agencies have been forced to close, and heterosexual couples have been denied the ability to adopt unless they are willing to support the homosexual agenda. It is my anticipation that if and when the homosexual movement gains sufficient power and influence in our country its members are likely to begin denouncing their opponents as bigots, to seek punishments such as jail sentences for Christians who publicly voice support for what St. Paul says about sodomy, to seek to ban bibles which continue to include the Pauline admonitions against sodomy and the Genesis account (Chap. 19) about the destruction of Sodom and Gomorrah, etc. There are already proposals for gay/lesbian history courses which would probably tend to glorify the gay/lesbian life-style, and proposals for fairy tales about two kings living and ruling together to replace fairy tales about a king and queen as a way to indoctrinate preschoolers into an acceptance of this lifestyle. The beginnings of these types of systematic indoctrination and persecution are already appearing in Europe. Every one, homosexual and straight alike, should acknowledge the fact that the Bible, which Christians accept as the inspired word of God, simply cannot be tampered with, and should never be blasphemed.

CONCLUDING REMARKS

In this article we have described and deplored the present status of sexual freedom and promiscuity that prevails in our culture, and we have called for a return to the stricter moral standards that prevailed a century ago. We have also argued against acknowledging homosexual unions as valid marriages since such recognition would be a step in the direction toward a further relaxation of traditional moral standards. We urge the passage of statewide and national constitutional amendments that define marriage as the union of one man and one woman as a way to resolve the question. We also fear the passage of laws that would criminalize the preaching of sermons by priests and ministers in support of what St. Paul says about sexual morality. Such a situation could be the beginning of a persecution of Christianity, and some European countries as well as Canada have been moving in this direction. It is an ominous possible eventuality. Fortunately, the Christian Church has survived far worse challenges in the past!

REPLY BY RON

The Unitarian point of view to controversial topics such as gay marriage is to consider them from the point of view of the participants. If no one gets hurt in the process, why should we object? In the case of gay marriage, the only likely problem lies in the benefits of marriage over celibacy. A married person has certain benefits, for example those that follow the decease of one of the partners. If we believe in the equality which our constitution demands, presumably we should accept arrangements between same sex couples as would occur in a more conventional marriage, so that the surviving partner would in fact benefit on the death of the other by the same amount irrespective of gender.

A few weeks ago I played the wedding march on my accordion for two female friends of mine who were getting married on the ocean beach. It was a moving ceremony. They had made a commitment to one another more than ten years previously, but no legal agreement was then possible. Now it was, and they were very happy about it.

Let us examine the social reasons for marriage. The original social purpose was to provide protection for the children born as a result of the marriage, although love between the partners is often given as the prime reason. However, love can die with time, but the kids remain, and should be given a happy childhood. In the past single women could rarely earn enough to provide adequate support.

Unlike the romantic weddings of today, marriage in ancient Rome was an arrangement between two families. Like much of Roman society, it was highly structured, but also logical and, in some ways, even modern. However, it had very little to do with religion, and much more to do with keeping wealth in the family. The partners were brought together by the families, so love had little to do with it. The same is true of the Hindu religion today, and much to my surprise, personal experience has shown me that such Hindu marriages are frequently very successful.

Ostensibly, our new laws concerning same sex marriage do not involve religion, since the separation of church and state was a fundamental basis of the constitution, and has proved of great value, in spite of attack by religions of various kinds, who might benefit by some form of state religion.

The public view on same sex marriage has changed dramatically over the past few years, as detailed by Charlie. The matter has now been legalized by the federal government.

One should be careful about edicts from the church. For example, although the Christian church now demands one wife, the Jews of ancient times had many - as witness their kings. The problems the Catholic Church has had recently with the sexual interaction of certain priests with their young males might well not have occurred had they been allowed to marry. Sex, like alcohol, has always been difficult to regulate.

NUMBER OF GENDERS

One of the problems of same sex marriage lies in the definition of "same sex". There are, of course the extremes, the conventional male-female relationship but also where two obviously male males (or females) fall in love. But what if a female who looks like a male falls for an obviously female

female? There is even a word for this - "butch" for the obviously male type female, and "dyke" for the female type female. So there is a continuous transition in both genders from male to female appearance, behavior and all other associated appurtenances. It used to be thought that one could change this with drugs or behavioral modification. Such ideas have long since vanished (except in certain religions!). So, if you are so inclined, you have to live with it – and, indeed, in many respects, it must be a burden in today's society - though less so than in the past. As a "normal" male I have often wondered what it is like to be "gay". Unlike other things, you cannot walk a mile in a gay person's shoes, because the problem lies in the mind, and is it really a problem, because it lies in our consciousness, and this cannot be altered until we learn how to alter this part of the genetic code. If I see a picture of Marilyn Monroe, I immediately react mentally - (this is what keeps "PLAYBOY" magazine alive!). But no male turns me on, whereas a "hunk" of a male affects a girl. What has all this got to do with same sex marriage? Unfortunately, marriage was created on the assumption that we were all "normal" males and females, a disastrous mistake. The acceptance of gay marriage has at least reduced some of the problems associated with the gay community, namely its acceptance by people in general.

Poole refers to a six-gender society. I doubt you could divide it so accurately - it seems to me to be a more continuous gradation between the sexes than that. Furthermore, society today is far more permissive than in the past. Part of this is due to two medical advances. One is "the Pill" the contraceptive device which allows intercourse without the risk of pregnancy. Erection enhancing drugs provided the second advance. This benefits those of us who are unable to "keep it up". Both of these must have increased the amount of sexual intercourse throughout the world by a vast amount- married or not! So we live in a far different world from our parents.

The rate of advance with digital electronic communication has made available to us the ability to communicate instantly throughout the world. The knowledge we accumulate has meant that such problems as gay marriage can be examined from a very different viewpoint, which has made them generally more acceptable, because of the clear satisfaction acceptance gives to the marriage partners.

END SEXUAL PREJUDICE

The benefits of social acceptance are now becoming obvious to the general public, where previously only the somewhat bigoted religious point of view was fed us. Hence it is likely same sex marriage is here with us to stay.

WHAT IS "NORMAL" SEXUALITY?

The American Psychiatric Associations definition of normality now includes homosexuality. This leads one to enquire what is meant by normality? It is true that a sizeable population of the world is born with homosexual proclivities, which are inherent and not easily changed-hence they will live with this proclivity - so to them this may well be normal.

SCRIPTURAL EDICTS

Christian scripture today is very definitive about what is allowed sexually - one man and one woman married. However, what actually occurs in the real world is somewhat different. It is becoming more and more popular for a couple to live together before marriage. Experience shows this to be a good thing - whereas a couple getting married before a trial is much more likely to split. It is much easier to split if you are not married, and less harm is done. Getting a divorce once married is far more difficult. Furthermore, it is quite possible for one partner to find he (or she) is homosexual after the marriage-and this really presents problems. Nevertheless, it is better for incompatible couples to part rather than stay married "for the sake of the children". In fact it is almost inevitable that the children know anyhow. So, it is better to treat the religious and secular parts of the marriage quite separately, if possible.

DOMINAMCE OF GAY COUPLES

Charlie points out that if gay couples become more socially acceptable, they may dominate society. This seems unlikely, given that they still make such a very small fraction of society. Nevertheless, we should accept them - this forms the basis of the Unitarian-Universalist church. Each of us holds the key to our own salvation - if you believe in salvation that is.

SEX AND THE INDIVIDUAL

Same sex marriage is nevertheless a product of sexual interaction though of a different nature than that we are used to, so it might be useful to see how sex fits in. At its lowest level, sex involves one individual-masturbation, an inevitable but not very satisfying product of life on earth. Next comes paid for sex-prostitution. Mostly, though not always, this involves opposite sexes. The regulation of prostitution has provided the salaries of law enforcement since time immemorial. The oldest profession is still going strong, and shows no signs of decreasing. Because of its temporary nature, there is no implication of marriage - in fact it is because of this that it is popular! In the past, in western countries it was common for couples to become engaged. Ostensibly, there was no intercourse until marriage, but who knows? The crest of sexual endeavor is marriage between two partners of opposite sex, culminating in children - in fact, it is the raising of children that is the ultimate aim of marriage. This is why same sex marriage is objected to - no children. However the adoption of children by gay parents is becoming more popular. It is clear parents of opposite sex may be preferable, but nevertheless, love between partners and children is the objective.

SEX AND POPULATION CONTROL

This may be a suitable point to introduce a problem for the future - overpopulation of the world. This is related to gay marriage because such marriages rarely involve children. The rate at which the population of the world is increasing means that within the next century it will become very difficult, if not impossible to provide food for them all. So far, increase in population has been met with new techniques to grow larger crops of staple foods, however this cannot go on forever. Gay marriage if it produces no children will at least provide some relief.

SEX AND THE LAW

Sex and the law have always been at odds. The most contentious issues involve death, and more recently, marriage. In the case of death, euthanasia sets a problem. Basically, should a person be kept alive by artificial means? Medical doctors take a conservative attitude. Afraid of being sued for very large sums of money by the patient's relatives if they do not, they keep the patient alive as long as possible, even if the brain is dead. This problem has an immediate solution for those who have made a living will. However for many the mere thought of death is repugnant, leaving the relatives with an awkward problem.

At the other extreme, although abortion is legal, it is fraught with severe restrictions. The worst problem arises with a deformed or otherwise nonviable fetus. Then comes the question, should you save the mother at the expense of the life of the fetus, or should you save the fetus, dooming the mother? So many issues arise here. For example, if the fetus is delivered, is it going to live a normal life, or is it going to have medical problems making it a burden to itself and society for its lifetime. Clearly, here we have ethical problems that would tax the mind of Socrates.

CONCLUSION

Public opinion is drifting in favor of same sex marriage, away from the more conservative attitude. It is likely this will go on for some time, but ultimately there will be a reaction to older standards. Such oscillations are bound to occur, but it is likely that slowly, some form of same sex marriage will gain acceptance. This will involve the constitution, which after all requires equality between different beliefs.

REFERENCES FOR MIRACLES

1. Joan Carroll Cruz, *The Incorruptibles*, Tan, Charlotte NC, 1977

2. Paul Glynn, *Healing Fire of Christ*, Ignatius, San Francisco, 1999

3. John Lochran, *The Miracle of Lourdes*, St. Anthony Messenger, Cincinnati, 2008.

4. Dan Lynch, *Our Lady of Guadalupe*, JKMI Press, St. Albans VT, 2004.

5. Joan Carroll Cruz, *Eucharistic Miracles*, Tan, Charlotte, NC, 1986.

6. *The Eucharistic Miracles of the World*, Eternal Life, Bardstown KY, 2009.

7. Michael Freze, *They Bore the Wounds of Christ*, Our Sunday Visitor, Huntington IN, 1989.

8. Ted Harrison, *Stigmata*, Penguin, New York, 1996.

9. Kenneth L. Woodward, *Making Saints*, Touchstone, New York, 1990.

10. Lynn Picknett and Clive Prince, *Turin Shroud*, Harper Collins, New York, 1994.

11. Harry E. Gove, *Relic, Icon or Hoax?*, Institute of Physics, Philadelphia, 1996.

12. Gilbert R. Lovie, *Unlocking the Secrets of the Shroud*, Thomas More, Allen TX, 1998.

BIBLIOGRAPHY FOR TRINITY

1. Joas Adiprasetya, *An Imaginative Glimpse, The Trinity and Multiple Participations.* Pickwick, Eugene OR, 2013.

2. Allen Coppedge, *The Triune God*, IVP Academic, Illinois, 2007.

3. Gilles Emery, O. P., *The Trinity*, Catholic Univ. of America Press, Washington DC, 2011.

4. Edmund J. Fortman, *The Triune God*, Wipf & Stock, Eugene OR, 1982.

5. Stanley J. Grenz, *Rediscovering the Triune God*, Fortress Press, Minneapolis, MN, 2004.

6. Gerald O'Collins, *The Tripersonal God*, Paulist, Mahwah NJ, 2014. Contains an excellent bibliography.

7, Roger E. Olson and Christopher A. Hall, *The Trinity*, Erdmans, Cambridge, UK, 2002.

8. Joseph Pohle, *The Divine Trinity*, Wipf & Stock, Eugene OR, 2010.

9. Karl Rahner, The Trinity, Crossroad, NY, 1967, vide esp. p. xi.

10. Gloria L. Schaab, CSJ, *Trinity in Relation*, Anselm Academic, Winona MN, 2012.

11. A. Edward Siecienski, *The Filioque, History of a Doctrinal Controversy*, Oxford UP, Oxford. 2010.

12. *Conciliorum Oecumenicorum Decreta*, Edizioni Dehoniane, Bologtna, Italy, 1973 (1991).

13. Ad. Tanquery, *Synopsis Theologiae Dogmaticae*, Vol. II, Desclèe, Tornaci, Belgium, 1922.

14. Mitch Stokes, *Isaac Newton*, Thomas Nelson, Nashville TN. 2010.

BIOGRAPHY

Ron Edge

Ron Edge, was born in a Lancashire mill town in England. His parents met working in a tannery, run by a Methodist family called Walker, so he was christened a Methodist. His mother was a shorthand typist there, and his father a laborer with a poor educational background. However, after tutoring by his wife, he became a clerk in local government. Growing up, his friends were Church of England, so he was confirmed in that faith.

Edge attended the local Council School, and was lucky enough to win a scholarship to Bolton School, a well-known Public School, (and therefore private by English tradition). He had a typical science education but we also had one religion class a week, led by a church of England minister. This was during the war so he must have had a medical problem. It was a unique class because the teacher allowed the students discuss their beliefs, and it set Edge's for his future, The teacher called himself a "Christian agnostic". Edge still believes the edicts of Christianity, but is dubious about the miracles!

He won a major scholarship to Queens' College Cambridge graduating BA, MA, (triple 1st class honors), and PhD from the Cavendish Laboratory Cambridge. Emigrating to Australia, he rebuilt an electron synchrotron from the Atomic Energy Research Establishment at Harwell at the Australian National University and researched there. His first marriage was in Australia, by a bishop of the Church of England in Australia (now the Anglican Church of Australia), the second marriage being at the Unitarian Universalist (UU) Winter institute in Florida, all leading to a varied religious background. Also, his first wife was Czech, and his second wife Danish.

GOD YES OR NO?

UNITARIAN UNIVERSALISM

The outcome is that he became a Unitarian, which allows one to make one's own religious decisions, since it has no creed. If in an elevator between floors someone asks "Unitarianism, what is that?" the following elevator definition is often given, "That is the 'no hell' church". In1952 the Unitarians joined with the Universalists. It is sometimes said the difference between the Unitarians and Universalists is that Universalists believe that God is too good to damn people, and Unitarians believe that people are too good to be damned.

In spite of the absence of creed, Unitarians are surprisingly uniform in their beliefs. The basic tenet is that there is only one God, the nature of which is not specified. Hence there is no Trinity to worry about. One can have agnostic views, saying, "I have no idea what God is like", or you can employ one of the Christian creeds, missing out the bits about the Virgin Birth, and the Ascension into heaven. You can even be an atheist with Unitarian views. The main point is that you have a belief.

US citizenship

Ron migrated to the United States where he taught and researched at the University of South Carolina, researching also at Oak Ridge and Los Alamos National Laboratories, Yale, Stanford, Sussex and Munich universities, the University of the Witwatersrand and the California Institute of Technology, subsequently becoming a US citizen.

He is a fellow of the American Physical Society, and was president and is a fellow of the American Association of Physics Teachers. He developed a series of television programs called "Science Talks", also introducing the Monte Python show on SCETV. He is past president of the Unitarian Universalist Fellowship of Columbia.

His hobby is church bell ringing, and he is a member of the Royal Cumberland Youths Society of Change Ringers.

BIOGRAPHY

Charles P. Poole, Jr.

I grew up in a typical middle class Catholic environment in Brooklyn. I had one sister, Nancy, two and a half years younger than myself. My father was a banker working at 55 Wall Street for the National City Bank of NY, which eventually became Citibank, and my mother was a housewife who stayed at home with her two children, as did most of the wives of our neighbors. We attended Mass every Sunday at our parish St. Gregory which had three or four priests in residence. There were nuns living in a nearby convent who staffed the parish grammar school which Nancy and I attended. We learned religion by memorizing answers to questions from the Baltimore Catechism. We both attended Catholic high schools.

During this grammar school/high school period my religious convictions were developing. I had come to the conclusion that the most important aspect of our heritage was the Scriptures so I embarked on a project to read the entire Bible. Since there are 1235 chapters (OT 979 + NT 256) in the Catholic Bible, reading a chapter a day not counting Sundays took 44.3 months or 3.69 years of effort. I embarked on this task in late grammar school, and completed it about half way through high school. None of my teachers were enthusiastic about this project, and they cautioned me to read all of the many footnotes to avoid falling into heresy. This I did, of course, and I learned a great deal from them. Whenever I was criticized for too much Bible reading I pointed out the inscription on the front page which assigned an indulgence for scripture reading. This silenced my critics. Later while in college at Fordham I read many of the ancient Christian writings such as the Didache, Polycarp, Iranaeus, and the Epistle of Barnabas which I found fascinating and very supportive of Catholicism. My teachers and priests

118

considered this reading program as rather weird and atypical for a young Catholic.

After graduating from Prep I decided to become a Jesuit priest so I entered the Novitiate St. Andrew on the Hudson where we spoke Latin and the emphasis was on much communal prayer. The highlight of the experience was the thirty-day silent retreat called the Spiritual Exercises of St. Ignatius, which consisted of five meditations every day. Before each meditation the retreat master spent half an hour presenting the novices with the topics to meditate on, and then we knelt meditating for an hour with a two-minute standing break half way through. Most of us developed calluses on our knees. The first week we meditated on the fundamentals of spirituality, and then on the public life of Jesus, the passion and death of Jesus, and finally on the resurrected life of Jesus. This was the greatest spiritual experience of my life. After seven months at St. Andrew on the Hudson I decided not to continue, so I returned to civilian life and enrolled in the pre-med program at Fordham University.

At Fordham I became very interested in social issues. I was especially influenced by the Pastoral Letter *Growth or Decline? The Church Today* written in 1947 by Emmanuel Cardinal Suhard, the Archbishop of Paris. It said on page 15, "It is not for her (the Church) to adapt her teaching, but for civilization to assimilate it." This is as true today as it was in 1947. I was also influenced by the ideas of Dorothy Day and Peter Maurin and I visited their establishment on Mott Street, Manhattan several times. Day proclaimed the mission "to live in accordance with the justice and charity of Jesus Christ" and their houses were well known for hospitality towards those on the margin of society. During the late 1940s and 1950s I spent a great deal of time at Friendship House a mission serving the poor Negros (African Americans) in a Harlem neighborhood. The poverty there was incredible. My favorite magazines were Integrity and Cross Currents, both of which emphasized the social mission of Christianity. I wondered why my parish St. Gregory had so little concern for these social issues, and they and my family wondered why I was so concerned about them. I also became a proponent for using English to say Mass and to administer sacraments like Baptism.

My fiancée Kathleen Walsh and I joined a street preaching group The Campaigners for Christ the King directed by Arthur Stabile who preached in Union Square, Manhattan, where the Communists were active. We eventually married and had five children and fifteen grand children.

In the 50s some friends and I visited many Christian pastors with the question, "Why is your denomination the best?" I learned a great deal about the diversity of Christianity and the ecumenical movement from these interviews. Later I made a study of the main documents of various denominations and religions such as the Lutheran Book of Concord, John Calvin's Institutes of the Christian Religion, the Book of Common Prayer, The Westminster Confession, the Analects of Confucius, the Hindu Upanishads, the Qur'an (Koran) and some Buddhist literature. Comments on the Christian documents and the Qur'an are posted on my website **www.faithseekingunderstanding.com** .

The Second Vatican Council, which was in session from 1962 to 1965, had two main aims often referred to as *aggiornamento* or updating the Church and *ad fontes,* *(i.e. resourcement)* or returning the Church to its sources. The first involves expressing the message of the Gospel in ways that conform to the mentality of various cultures, with much attention given to social issues. We now accept Protestants as fellow Christians, and offer our Masses and Sacraments in vernacular languages. The second aim meant becoming a Scripture-based people like many Protestants. The Council thus changed the Church in just the way I wanted it to, so I became a conservative anxious for the implementation but opposed to further changes.

After graduating from Fordham and failing to gain entrance into Medical School I obtained an MS in Physics from Fordham and then a doctorate in Physics from the University of Maryland. After this I sent six years doing research at the Gulf Oil Company in Pittsburgh, and the remainder of my career on the faculty of Physics at the University of South Carolina.